BOOKKEEPING EXERCISES
FOR JUNIOR CERTIFICATE

BOOKKEEPING EXERCISES FOR JUNIOR CERTIFICATE

Patrick Collins

Gill & Macmillan

Gill & Macmillan Ltd
Goldenbridge
Dublin 8
with associated companies throughout the world
www.gillmacmillan.ie

© Patrick Collins 2000
0 7171 3058 4
Print origination in Ireland by Carole Lynch

*The paper used in this book is made from the wood pulp of
managed forests. For every tree felled, at least one tree is planted,
thereby renewing natural resources.*

Solutions to questions in this book are
available at:
www.gillmacmillan.ie/bookkpex

Contents

Chapter 1
Double-Entry Bookkeeping

Double-Entry Bookkeeping is so called because each transaction is recorded twice — first in the Cash Book and then in the relevant account for that particular item e.g. Sales Account, Purchases Account, ESB Account, Insurance Account etc.

1.1 Cash Book

The Cash Book, also known as the Bank Account, has two sides:
a Debit (DR)Side and a Credit (CR)Side.

All entries in the Cash Book refer only to money spent or received.

Monies or cheques received by the business are recorded on the debit side. Money spent or payments made by cheque are recorded on the credit side.
Note: Credit transactions i.e. Credit Sales, Credit Purchases are not entered in the Cash Book.

FIGURE 1 — LAYOUT OF CASH BOOK

DR			Cash Book		CR
	Cash	Bank		Cash	Bank
Money Received			Money Spent		

If an entry is on the debit side of the Cash Book then the entry in the relevant account will be on the credit side. This is known as Double-Entry Bookkeeping and ensures the accuracy of the accounts.

All entries in the Cash Book refer only to money spent or received.

The Cash Book may also have an opening balance of cash in cash column/money in bank in bank column.

1.2 Ledgers

The accounts are kept in three books called ledgers.

1. **General Ledger (GL)** for general entries including assets, liabilities, expenses and revenue accounts.
2. **Debtors Ledger (DL)** for money received from debtors (people who owe money to the business).
3. **Creditors Ledger (CL)** for payments to creditors (people to whom the business owes money).

FOLIOS

A folio reference indicates where to find the corresponding debit and credit entries once they have been transferred from the Cash Book to the relevant accounts in the three ledgers. The first two letters of the folio reference refer to the type of ledger the account can be found in. The number reference indicates the page number of the other account involved in the transaction.

Worked Example I

Ian McCarthy had €50 cash held in the business on 1 January 1996 and €750 in the business bank account.

Record the following cash/cheque transactions in the Cash Book. VAT is 10% on sales and purchases.

01 Jan. Cash Sales lodged €750.
02 Jan. Paid ESB by cheque €260.
03 Jan. Purchased goods by cheque €400.
05 Jan. Cash Sales lodged €600.
06 Jan. Received €180 from debtor Tim Murphy by cheque.
07 Jan. Paid insurance by cheque €200.
09 Jan. Cash Sales €140.
10 Jan. Cash Purchases €150.

Table 01 — Cash Book of Ian McCarthy

DR								Cash Book							CR
Date	Particulars	Folio	Cash Sales	Other Receipts	VAT	Cash	Bank	Date	Particulars	Folio	Cash Purchases	Other Payments	VAT	Cash	Bank
01 Jan.	Balance	b/d				50	750	02 Jan.	ESB	FL2		260			260
01 Jan.	Sales	GL1	750		75		825	03 Jan.	Purchases	GL3	400		40		440
05 Jan.	Sales	GL1	600		60		660	07 Jan.	Insurance	GL4		200			200
06 Jan.	T. Murphy	DL1		180			180	10 Jan.	Purchases	GL3	150		15	165	
09 Jan.	Sales	GL1	140		14	154									

1.3 Balancing the Account

Add up all entries in the Cash Column on both sides and calculate the difference.
   Add up all entries in Bank Column and calculate the difference.
   The difference is shown on the credit side as the Balance Carried Down (Balance c/d) to the following month.

Worked Example II

Find the balance of Ian McCarthy's account as at 10 Jan.

Cash Column Debit Side:	€50 + €154 = €204
Cash Column Credit Side:	€165
	€39DR is the difference.

The business will therefore begin February with €39 Balance Brought Down (Balance b/d) from January.

Bank Column Debit Side	€2,415
Credit Side	€900
	€1515 is the difference

Table 02 — Cash Book
Finding Cash and Bank Balances

DR			Cash Book		CR
	Total Cash	**Total Bank**		**Total Cash**	**Total Bank**
Dr Total Cash and Bank	204	2,415	Cr Total Cash and Bank	165	900
			Balance	39	1,515
	204	2,415		204	2,415

Guide to Students:

Tables 01 and 02 are given as step stages to showing Table 03 which shows that Ian McCarthy has €39 cash and €1,515 in his Bank Account at the end of January, beginning of February.

Table 03 — The Balanced Cash Book of Ian McCarthy

CR							Cash Book								DR
Date	Particulars	F	Cash Sales	Other Receipts	VAT	Cash	Bank	Date	Particulars	F	Cash Purchases	Other Payments	VAT	Cash	Bank
01 Jan.	Balance	b/d				50	750	02 Jan.	ESB	GL2		260			260
01 Jan.	Sales	GL1	750		75		825	03 Jan.	Purchases	GL3	400		40		440
05 Jan.	Sales	GL1	600		60		660	07 Jan.	Insurance	GL4		200			200
06 Jan.	T. Murphy	DL1		180			180	10 Jan.	Purchases	GL3	150		15	165	
09 Jan.	Sales	GL1	140		14	154		31 Jan.	Balance	c/d				39	1,515
			1490	180	149	204	2,415				550	460	55	204	2,415
01 Feb.	Balance	b/d				39	1,515								

Table 04 — The Balanced Accounts of Ian McCarthy for January

GENERAL LEDGER

DR			Sales Account (1)	Date	Particulars	F	CR
Date	Particulars	F	Amount	Date	Particulars	F	Amount
				01 Jan.	Bank	CB	750
				05 Jan.	Bank	CB	600
				09 Jan.	Cash	CB	140
							1,490

DR			ESB Account (2)				CR
02 Jan.	Bank	CB	260				

DR			Purchases Account (3)				CR
03 Jan.	Bank	CB	400				
10 Jan.	Cash	CB	150				
			550				

DR			Insurance Account (4)				CR
07 Jan.	Bank	CB	200				

DR			VAT Account (5)				CR
31 Jan.	Cash Purchases	CB	55	31 Jan.	Cash Sales		149
31 Jan.	Balance	c/d	94				
		149	149				149
				01 Feb.	Balance	b/d	94

DR					T. Murphy's Account (1)			CR
					06 Jan.	Bank	CB	180

Note: The figure transferred from the Cash Book to the Sales Account or Purchases Account is the amount for purchases and sales without VAT.

VAT charged on sales is owed by the business to the Revenue Commissioners less the amount paid on purchases.

Example and Questions on Cash Book and Ledgers

Worked Example III

Owen Keane had €50 cash in his business on 1 February 1999 and €450 in the business bank account.

Enter the following cash/cheque transactions in the Cash Book and then transfer the entries from the Cash Book to the ledger. VAT is 10% on purchases and sales.

01 Feb. Cash Sales lodged €700.
02 Feb. Purchased goods by cash €100.
03 Feb. Purchased office stationery by cash €20.
04 Feb. Paid insurance by cheque €360.
05 Feb. Cash Sales €200.
06 Feb. Cash Sales lodged €400.
07 Feb. Purchased goods by cheque €250.

Table 05 – Cash Book of Owen Keane for Feb. 1999

DR								Cash Book							CR
Date	Particulars	F	Cash Sales	Other Receipts	VAT	Cash	Bank	Date	Particulars	F	Cash Purchases	Other Payments	VAT	Cash	Bank
01 Feb.	Balance	b/d				50	450	02 Feb.	Purchases	GL2	100		10	110	
01 Feb.	Sales	GL1	700		70		770	03 Feb.	Stationery	GL3		20		20	
05 Feb.	Sales	GL1	200		20	220		04 Feb.	Insurance	GL4		360			360
06 Feb.	Sales	GL1	400		40		440	07 Feb.	Purchases	GL2	250		25		275
								07 Feb.	Balance	c/d				140	1,025
			1,300		130	270	1,660				350	380	35	270	1,660
08 Feb.	Balance	b/d				140	1,025								

Table 06 — Ledgers of Owen Keane

GENERAL LEDGER

DR					Sales Account (1)			CR
					01 Feb.	Bank	CB	700
					05 Feb.	Cash	CB	200
					06 Feb.	Bank	CB	400
								1,300

DR				Purchases Account (2)				CR
02 Feb.	Cash	CB	100					
07 Feb.	Bank	CB	250					
			350					

DR				Stationery Account(3)				CR
03 Feb.	Cash	CB	20					

DR				Insurance Account (4)				CR
04 Feb.	Bank	CB	360					

DR				VAT Account (5)				CR
07 Feb.	Total Cash Purchases		350	07 Feb.	Total Cash Sales	CB	130	
				07 Feb.	Balance	c/d	220	
			350				350	
08 Feb		c/d	220					

Practice Questions

In the following questions you are required to:
(A) Enter the listed transactions in the Cash Book.
(B) Transfer the entries from the Cash Book to the ledgers.

1. Shane Burke had €160 cash in his business on 1 February 1996 and €450 in the business bank account.

    The following cash/cheque transactions took place during the month of February. VAT is 10% on purchases and sales of stock.

    Feb. 1 Cash Sales lodged €800.

    Feb. 2 Paid insurance €240 by cheque.

    Feb. 3 Purchased goods by cash €200.

    Feb. 4 Paid for office stationery €20 cash.

Feb. 5 Cash Sales €150.
Feb. 6 Purchased goods by cheque €200.
Feb. 7 Cash Sales lodged €250.

2. Pat Galvin had €70 cash in his business on 1 March 1996 and €950 in his business bank account.
    The following cash/cheque transactions took place during the month of March. VAT is 10% on purchases and sales of stock.

    01 Mar. Cash Purchases €150.
    02 Mar. Cash Sales €200.
    03 Mar. Paid Car Tax by cheque €150.
    04 Mar. Purchased computer for office by cheque €1,200 (no VAT).
    05 Mar. Cash Sales lodged €700.
    06 Mar. Cash Sales lodged €900.
    07 Mar. Paid for light, heat by cheque €240.

3. Mary O'Callaghan had €150 cash in her business 1 April 1996 and €800 in her business bank account.
    The following cash/cheque transactions took place during the month of April. VAT is 10% on purchases and sales of stock.

    01 Apr. Cash Sales lodged €500.
    03 Apr. Cash Purchases €150.
    04 Apr. Purchased goods by cheque €400.
    05 Apr. Paid for repairs to machinery by cheque €200.
    06 Apr. Cash Sales €400.
    07 Apr. Paid for rent by cheque €200.
    10 Apr. Cash Sales lodged €600.
    11 Apr. Cash Sales €200.

4. Sandra O'Sullivan had €200 cash in her business on 1 May 1996 and €1,200 in her business bank account.
    The following cash/cheque transactions took place during the month of May. VAT is 10% on purchases and sales of stock.

    01 May Cash Sales €150.
    03 May Cash Sales lodged €700.
    04 May Purchased goods by cheque €200.
    05 May Paid insurance by cheque €150.
    06 May Purchased stationery by cash €50 (no VAT).
    07 May Cash Sales €100.
    08 May Paid wages by cheque €400.

5. Carmel O'Rourke had €60 cash in her business on 1 June 1996 and €800 in her business bank account.

    The following cash/cheque transactions took place during the month of June. VAT is 10% on purchases and sales of stock.

    01 June Paid wages by cheque €200.
    02 June Purchased goods by cheque €300.
    03 June Cash Sales €250.
    04 June Cash Sales lodged €600.
    05 June Paid insurance by cheque €250.
    06 June Cash Purchases €150
    07 June Cash Sales lodged €350.

6. Paul Geary had €70 cash in his business on 1 July 1996 and €750 in his business bank account.

    The following cash/cheque transactions took place during the month of July. VAT is 10% on purchases and sales of stock.

    01 July Purchased office equipment by cheque €4,000 (no VAT).
    02 July Paid car and van insurance by cheque €1,400.
    03 July Cash Sales lodged €1,600.
    04 July Purchased goods by cheque €800.
    05 July Paid for advertising €60 cash.
    06 July Cash Sales lodged €2,000.
    Note: Bank overdraft at end of July in Cash Book i.e. Balance c/d 31 July on debit side.

7. Una Brennan had €160 cash in her business on 1 August 1996 and €840 in her business bank account.

    The following cash/cheque transactions took place during the month of August. VAT is 10% on purchases and sales of stock.

    01 Aug. Cash Sales lodged €400.
    02 Aug. Paid wages by cheque €360.
    03 Aug. Cash Sales €50.
    04 Aug. Purchased goods by cheque €400.
    05 Aug. Cash Sales lodged €900.
    06 Aug. Purchased office equipment €250 by cheque (no VAT).
    07 Aug. Cash Purchases €100.

8. Kieran Ryan had €80 cash in his business on 1 September 1996 and a bank overdraft of €490 (i.e. Credit Cash Book bank balance).

The following cash/cheque transactions took place during the month of September. VAT 10% is charged on purchases and sales of stock.

01 Sept. Cash Sales lodged €3,900.
02 Sept. Purchased goods by cheque €2,000.
03 Sept. Cash Sales €200.
04 Sept. Paid wages by cheque €450.
05 Sept. Paid insurance by cheque €600.
06 Sept. Cash Sales lodged €2,500.
07 Sept. Purchased stationery €80 by cheque.

9. Breda Walsh had €150 cash in her business on 1 October 1996 and €2,100 in her business bank account.
   The following cash/cheque transactions took place during the month of October. VAT is 10% on purchases and sales of stock.

01 Oct. Cash Sales lodged €1,500.
02 Oct. Paid rent by cheque €400.
03 Oct. Purchased goods by cheque €1,000.
04 Oct. Paid advertising €80 cash.
05 Oct. Cash Sales lodged €1,200.
06 Oct. Purchased motor van by cheque €8,000 (no VAT).
07 Oct. Cash Sales €250.

10. John Fitzgerald had €200 cash in his business on 1 November 1996 and a bank overdraft of €2,200.
    The following cash/cheque transactions took place during the month of November. VAT is 10% on purchases and sales of stock.

01 Nov. Purchased motor van by cheque €16,000 (no VAT).
02 Nov. Cash Sales lodged €5,400.
03 Nov. Paid insurance by cheque €1,800.
04 Nov. Purchased goods by cheque €4,000.
05 Nov. Cash Sales lodged €9,000.
06 Nov. Cash Sales €300.
07 Nov. Paid telephone bill by cheque €200.

1.4 Credit Transactions

Goods sold on credit are entered in the Sales Book. Goods purchased on credit are entered in the Purchases Book. Goods sold or purchased on credit that are subsequently returned are entered in the Sales Returns Book or the Purchases Returns Book respectively.

Worked Example IV

Record the following transactions of Mitchell Ltd in the Sales Book, Purchases Book and Returns Book and post to the ledgers. VAT is 10% on all transactions.

01 Feb. Purchased goods on credit from D. Mulcahy €6,000
02 Feb. Sold goods on credit to T. Kiely €3,000.
03 Feb. Sold goods on credit to C. Morrissey €9,000.
06 Feb. C. Morrissey returned goods €1,000.
08 Feb. Purchased goods on credit from D. Murphy €4,000.
09 Feb. Returned goods to D. Murphy €2,000.

Table 05 — The Books of Mitchell Ltd for February

SALES BOOK

Date	Particulars	F	Details	Amount Credit Sales	VAT	Invoice Total
02 Feb.	T. Kiely	DL1		3,000	300	3,300
03 Feb.	C. Morrissey	DL2		9000	900	9,900
28 Feb.		GL1		12,000	1,200	13,200

PURCHASES BOOK

Date	Particulars	F	Details	Amount Credit Purchases	VAT	Invoice Total
01 Feb.	D. Mulcahy	CL1		6,000	600	6,600
08 Feb.	D. Murphy	CL2		4,000	400	4,400
28 Feb.		GL2		10,000	1,000	11,000

SALES RETURNS BOOK

Date	Particulars	F	Details	Amount	VAT	Credit Note Total
06 Feb.	C. Morrissey	DL1		1,000	100	1,100
28 Feb.		GL3		1,000	100	1,100

PURCHASES RETURNS BOOK

Date	Particulars	F	Details	Amount	VAT	Credit Note Total
09 Feb.	D. Murphy	CL2		2,000	200	2,200
28 Feb.		GL4		2,000	200	2,200

Table 06 — The Balanced Accounts of Mitchell Ltd for February

GENERAL LEDGER

DR				Sales Account (1)				CR
				28 Feb.	Sundry Debtors	SB	12,000	

DR				Purchases Account (2)				CR
28 Feb.	Sundry Creditors	PB	10,000					

DR				Sales Returns Account (3)				CR
28 Feb.	Sundry Debtors	SRB	1,000					

DR				Purchases Returns Account (4)				CR
				28 Feb.	Sundry Creditors	PRB	2,000	

DR				VAT Account (5)				CR
28 Feb.	Total Credit Purchases	PB	1,000	28 Feb.	Total Credit Sales	SB	1,200	
28 Feb.	Total Sales Returns	SRB	100	28 Feb.	Total Purchases Return	PRB	200	
28 Feb.	Balance	c/d	300					
			1,400				1,400	
				01 Mar.	Balance	b/d	300	

DEBTORS LEDGER

DR   **T. Kiely's Account (1)**   **CR**

02 Feb.	Sales	SB	3,300				

DR   **C. Morrissey's Account (2)**   **CR**

03 Feb.	Sales	SB	9,900	06 Feb	Sales Returns	SRB	1,100
				28 Feb.	Balance	c/d	8,800
			9,900				9,900
01 Mar.	Balance	b/d	8,800				

CREDITORS LEDGER

DR   **D. Mulcahy's Account (1)**   **CR**

				01 Feb.	Purchases	PB	6,600

DR   **D. Murphy's Account (2)**   **CR**

09 Feb.	Purchases Returns	PRB	2,200	08 Feb.	Purchases	PB	4,400
28 Feb.	Balance	c/d	2,200				
			4,400				4,400
				01 Mar.	Balance	b/d	2,200

Notes.

1. The total from the Sales Book is transferred to the credit side of the Sales Account as Sundry Debtors (the collection of Debtors). The amount transferred to the Sales Account is the amount without VAT.

   The amount of VAT is transferred to the VAT Account (credit side).

2. The totals from the Purchases Books and Returns Books are transferred to the corresponding accounts, again without VAT.

3. The credit entry in the Sales Account combined with the Credit Entry in the VAT Account for Sales is matched by debit entries in the accounts of the Debtors Ledger. The debit entries in the Debtors Ledger Accounts means these accounts now have debit balances.

4. The amounts transferred to the accounts in the Debtors and Creditors Ledgers are the gross amounts including VAT.

1.5 Trial Balance

The balance of each account at the end of the month is transferred to the same column of a Trial Balance.

The Trial Balance can be used when preparing the business's final accounts at the end of the year i.e. Trading Account, Profit and Loss Account and Balance Sheet.

The Trial Balance is a check on the accuracy of the double-entry system.

Worked Example V

Record the following transactions of Brown Ltd for May 2000 in the Books of First/Original Entry (Sales Book, Purchases Book and Returns Books) and post to the ledgers. Then transfer the balances from the ledgers to the Trial Balance. VAT is charged at 10% on all transactions.

01 Jan. Purchased goods on credit from G. Henderson €6,000.
02 Jan. Sold goods on credit to J. Cooney €8,000.
03 Jan. Returned goods to G. Henderson €1,000.
04 Jan. Sold goods on credit to C. Redmond €12,000.
05 Jan. Sales Returns €1,500 from J. Cooney.
06 Jan. Purchased goods on credit from J. Leahy €7,000.

Table 07 — The Books of Brown Ltd for January 1999

BOOKS OF FIRST ENTRY

Purchases Book						
Date	Particulars	F	Details	Purchases	VAT	Invoice Total
01 Jan.	G. Henderson	CL1		6,000	600	6,600
06 Jan.	J. Leahy	CL2		7,000	700	7,700
				13,000	1,300	14,300

Sales Book						
Date	Particulars	F	Details	Sales	VAT	Invoice Total
02 Jan.	J. Cooney	DL1		8,000	800	8,800
04 Jan.	C. Redmond	DL2		12,000	1,200	13,200
				20,000	2,000	22,000

Purchases Returns Book						
Date	Particulars	F	Details	Purchases Returns	VAT	Credit Note Total
03 Jan.	G. Henderson	CL1		1,000	100	1,100
				1,000	100	1,100

Sales Returns Book						
Date	Particulars	F	Details	Sales Returns	VAT	Credit Note Total
05 Jan.	J. Cooney	DL1		1,500	150	1,650
				1,500	150	1,650

GENERAL LEDGER

DR   **Purchases Account (1)**   **CR**

31 Jan.	Sundry Creditors	PB	13,000					

DR   **Sales Account (2)**   **CR**

				31 Jan.	Sundry Debtors	PB	20,000

DR   **Purchases Returns Account (3)**   **CR**

				31 Jan.	Sundry Creditors	PRB	1,000

DR   **Sales Returns Account (4)**   **CR**

31 Jan.	Sundry Debtors	SRB	1,500				

DR   **VAT Account (5)**   **CR**

31 Jan.	Total Credit Purchases	PB	1,300	31 Jan.	Total Credit Sales	SB	2,000
31 Jan.	Total Sales Returns	SRB	150	31 Jan.	Total Purchases Returns	PRB	100
31 Jan.	Balance	c/d	650				
			2,100				2,100
				01 Feb.	Balance	b/d	650

CREDITORS LEDGER

DR G. Henderson's Account (1) **CR**

03 Jan.	Purchases Returns	PRB	1,100	01 Jan.	Purchases	PB	6,600
31 Jan.	Balance	c/d	5,500				
			6,600				€6,600
				01 Feb.	Balance	b/d	5,500

DR J. Leahy's Account (2) **CR**

				06 Jan.	Purchases	PB	7,700

DEBTORS LEDGER

DR J. Cooney's Account (1) **CR**

02 Jan.	Sales	SB	8,800	05 Jan.	Sales Returns	SRB	1,650
				31 Jan.	Balance c/d		7,150
			8,800				8,800
01 Feb.	Balance	b/d	7,150				

DR C. Redmond's Account (2) **CR**

04 Jan.	Sales	SB	13,200				
			13,200				

TRIAL BALANCE AS AT 31 JANUARY 1999

	DR	CR
Purchases	13,000	
Sales		20,000
Purchases Returns		1,000
Sales Returns	1,500	
VAT		650
Creditors: G. Henderson		5,500
J. Leahy		7,700
Debtors: J. Cooney	7,150	
C. Redmond	13,200	
	34,850	34,850

Example and Questions on Sales Book, Purchases Book and Returns Book

In Questions 1-11 below record the transactions in the **Books of First Entry (Sales Book, Purchases Book and Returns Books)** and post to the ledgers. Then transfer the balances from the ledger to the Trial Balance at the end of each month. VAT of 10% is charged on all transactions.

1.
01 Jan. Purchased goods on credit from T. McCarthy €7,000.
02 Jan. Sold goods on credit to N. English €6,000.
03 Jan. Sales Returns €1,000 from N. English.
04 Jan. Sold goods on credit to P. Dunne €11,000.
05 Jan. Purchased goods on credit from J. Cooney €4,000.
06 Jan. Returned goods to J. Cooney €1,000.

2.
01 Feb. Purchased goods on credit from J. Wall €4,000.
02 Feb. Returned goods €1,000 to J. Wall €1,000.
03 Feb. Purchased goods on credit €2,000 from V. Lynch.
04 Feb. Sold goods on credit €9,000 to B. McCormack.
05 Feb. Sales Returns €1,000 from B. McCormack.
06 Feb. Sold goods on credit to J. Price €4,000.

3.
01 Mar. Sold goods on credit to S. Burke €3,000.
02 Mar. Purchased goods on credit from T. Stack €4,000.
03 Mar. Returned goods to T. Stack €1,000.
04 Mar. Sold goods on credit to P. Murray €5,000.
05 Mar. P. Murray returned goods €1,500.
06 Mar. Purchased goods on credit from A. Lonergan €2,000.

4.
02 Apr. Sold goods on credit to N. Fenton €4,000.
03 Apr. Sold goods on credit to J. Daly €7,000.
04 Apr. Sales Returns €3,000 from J. Daly.
05 Apr. Purchased goods on credit from W. Hayes €5,000.
06 Apr. Returned goods €500 to W. Hayes.
07 Apr. Purchased goods on credit from B. Power €1,500.

5.

01 May Sold goods on credit to J. Drummey €9,000.

02 May J. Drummey returned goods €500.

03 May Purchased goods on credit P. Power €3,000.

04 May Returned goods to P. Power €600.

05 May Sold goods on credit to P. Moore €5,000.

06 May Purchased goods on credit from R. Tobin €5,000.

6.

01 June Purchased goods on credit from C. Power €3,000.

02 June Had purchases returns from C. Power €400.

03 June Sold goods on credit to D. McGrath €18,000.

04 June D. McGrath returned goods €1,000.

05 June Purchased goods on credit from C. Wall €2,000.

06 June Sold goods on credit to D. Roche €5,000.

7.

01 July Purchased goods on credit from J. Power €4,000.

02 July Sold goods on credit to P. Lenane €9,000.

03 July Sold goods on credit to T. Osborne €10,000.

04 July P. Lenane returned goods €1,500.

05 July Purchased goods on credit from A. Fitzgerald €5,000.

06 July Returned goods to A. Fitzgerald €700.

8.

01 Aug. Sold goods on credit to E. Fitzpatrick €12,000.

02 Aug. Purchased goods on credit from K. Hoggarth €5,000.

03 Aug. E. Fitzpatrick returned goods €2,000.

04 Aug. Sold goods on credit to B. Lynch €7,000.

05 Aug. Purchased goods on credit from W. Hennebry €4,000.

06 Aug. Returned goods to W. Hennebry €3,000.

9.

01 Sept. Purchased goods on credit from S. O Hartaigh €5,000.

02 Sept. Sold goods on credit to D. O Murchadha €7,000.

03 Sept. Sold goods on credit to J. Houlihan €12,000.

04 Sept. Sales Returns from J. Houlihan €400.

05 Sept. Purchased goods on credit from S. Sanford €3,500.

06 Sept. Returned goods to S. Sanford €200.

10.

01 Oct. Sold goods on credit to K. Organ €8,000.

02 Oct. Purchased goods on credit from P. Veale €5,000.

03 Oct. Returned goods to P. Veale €600.

04 Oct. Sold goods on credit to P. Keating €6,000.

05 Oct. Sales Returns €400 from P. Keating.

06 Oct. Purchased goods on credit from D. Ryan €10,000.

11.

01 Nov. Sold goods on credit to D. Molloy €12,000.

02 Nov. D. Molloy returned goods €1,500.

03 Nov. Purchased goods on credit from R. Kirby €6,000.

04 Nov. Returned goods to R. Kirby €500.

05 Nov. Sold goods on credit to K. Crotty €8,000.

06 Nov. Purchased goods on credit from E. Kelly €3,000.

1.6 General Journal

The General Journal is used for recording entries which cannot be entered in any other books of 1st entry. Among entries recorded in the General Journal are the Opening Entries [the assets and liabilities in a business at the start of a year].

The purchase and sale of Fixed Assets is also recorded in the General Journal.

Worked Example VI

G. Nagle's business had the following assets and liabilities on 1 March 1996:
Premises €50,000, Motor Vehicles €20,000, Stock €3,000, Cash €60, Bank €3,600.
Debtors: D. Mulcahy €4,000, P. Morgan €6,000.
Creditors: J. Coffey €2,500, P. Lynch €4,500.
Share Capital €79,660.

(A) Record these opening balances in the General Journal and post the balances to the relevant ledger accounts.

(B) Write up the following transactions in the books of original/first entry i.e. Sales Book, Purchases Book, Returns Book and Cash Book, post to the ledgers and prepare a trial balance as at 31 May 1996. VAT is 10% on purchases, sales and returns.

01 Mar. Purchased goods on credit from J. Coffey €4,000.

07 Mar. Paid wages by cheque €800.

11 Mar. Cash Sales lodged €1,400.

13 Mar. Returned to P. Lynch €2,000 worth of goods.

16 Mar. Paid P. Lynch €11,000 by cheque.

17 Mar. Sold goods on credit to D. Mulcahy €12,000.

18 Mar. Sales Returns €3,000 from D. Mulcahy.

20 Mar. Received a cheque €10,500 from D. Mulcahy.

21 Mar. Cash Sales €1,700.

22 Mar. Paid advertising in cash €400.

23 Mar. Sold goods on credit to P. Morgan €3,000.

28 Mar. Received a cheque of €4,000 from P. Morgan.

Table 08 — General Journal of G. Nagle for March 1996

GENERAL JOURNAL

Date	Particulars		F	DR	CR
01 Mar.	Premises		GL1	50,000	
	Motor Vehicles		GL2	20,000	
	Stock		GL3	3,000	
	Cash		CB	60	
	Bank		CB	3,600	
	Debtors:	D. Mulcahy	DL1	4,000	
		P. Morgan	DL2	6,000	
	Creditors:	J. Coffey	CL1		2,500
		P. Lynch	CL2		4,500
	Share Capital		GL4		79,660
				86,660	86,660
	Being assets, liabilities and share capital on this date.				

Table 09 — Books of First Entry of Graham Nagle for March 1996

PURCHASES BOOK

Date	Particulars	F	Details	Purchases	VAT Total	Invoice
01 Mar.	J. Coffey	CL1		4,000	400	4,400
12 Mar.	P. Lynch	CL2		10,000	1,000	11,000
31 Mar.		GL5		14,000	1,400	15,400

SALES BOOK

Date	Particulars	F	Details	Sales	VAT	Invoice Total
17 Mar.	D. Mulcahy	DL1		12,000	1,200	13,200
23 Mar.	P. Morgan	DL2		3,000	300	3,300
31 Mar.		GL6		15,000	1,500	16,500

PURCHASES RETURNS BOOK

Date	Particulars	F	Details	Purchases Returns	VAT	Credit Note Total
13 Mar.	P. Lynch	CL2		2,000	200	2,200
31 Mar.		GL7		2,000	200	2,200

SALES RETURNS BOOK

Date	Particulars	F	Details	Sales Returns	VAT	Credit Note Total
18 Mar.	D. Mulcahy	DL1		3,000	300	3,300
	GL8			3,000	300	3,300

Table 10 — Cash Book of G. Nagle

DR								Cash Book							CR
Date	Particulars	F	Cash Sales	Other Receipts	VAT	Cash	Bank	Date	Particulars	F	Cash Purchases	Other Payments	VAT	Cash	Bank
01 Mar.	Balance	J				60	3,600	07 Mar.	Wages	GL9		800			800
11 Mar.	Sales	GL6	1,400		140		1,540	16 Mar.	P. Lynch	CL2	11,000				11,000
20 Mar.	D. Mulcahy	DL1		10,500			10,500	22 Mar.	Advertising	GL10		400		400	
21 Mar.	Sales	GL6	1,700		170	1,870		31 Mar.	Balance	c/d				1,530	7,840
28 Mar.	P. Morgan	DL2		4,000			4,000								
			3,100	14,500	310	1,930	19,640				12,200			1,930	19,640
01 Apr.	Balance	b/d				1,530	7,840								

Table 11 — Ledgers of G. Nagle

DR			Premises Account (1)					CR
01 Mar.	Balance	J	50,000					

DR			Motor Vehicles Account (2)					CR
01 Mar.	Balance	J	20,000					

DR			Stock Account (3)					CR
01 Mar.	Balance	J	3,000					

DR			Share Capital Account (4)					CR
					01 Mar.	Balance	J	79,660

DR			Purchases Account (5)					CR
31 Mar.	Sundry Creditors	PB	14,000					

DR			Sales Account (6)					CR
					11 Mar.	Bank	CB	1,400
					21 Mar.	Cash	CB	1,700
					31 Mar.	Sundry Debtors	SB	15,000
								18,100

DR			Purchases Returns Account (7)					CR
					31 Mar.	Sundry Creditors	PRB	2,000

DR			Sales Returns Account (8)					CR
31 Mar.	Sundry Debtors	SRB	3,000					

DR			Wages Account (9)					CR
07 Mar.	Bank	CB	800					

DR	Advertising Account (10)							CR
22 Mar.	Cash	CB	400					

DR	VAT Account(11)							CR
31 Mar.	Total Credit Purchases	PB	1,400	31 Mar.	Total Credit Sale	SB	1,500
31 Mar.	Total Sales Returns	SRB	300	31 Mar.	Total Purchase Return	PRB	200
31 Mar.	Balance	c/d	310	31 Mar.	Total Cash Sale		310
			1,840				1,840
					Balance	b/d	310

CREDITORS LEDGER

DR	J. Coffey's Account (1)							CR
				01 Mar.	Balance	J	2,500
				01 Mar.	Purchases	PB	4,400
							6,900

DR	P. Lynch's Account (2)							CR
13 Mar.	Purchases Returns	PRB	2,200	01 Mar.	Balance	J	4,500
16 Mar.	Bank	CB	11,000	12 Mar.	Purchases	PB	11,000
31 Mar.	Balance	c/d	2,300				
			15,500				15,500
				01 Apr.	Balance	b/d	2,300

DEBTORS LEDGER

DR	D. Mulcahy's Account (1)							CR
01 Mar.	Balance	J	4,000	18 Mar.	Sales Returns	SRB	3,300
17 Mar.	Sales	SB	13,200	20 Mar.	Bank	CB	10,500
				31 Mar.	Balance	c/d	3,400
			17,200				17,200
01 Apr.	Balance	b/d	3,400				

DR	P. Morgan's Account (2)						CR	
01 Mar.	Balance	J	6,000	28 Mar.	Bank	CB	4,000	
23 Mar.	Sales	SB	3,300	31 Mar.	Balance	c/d	5,300	
			9,300				9,300	
01 Apr.	Balance	b/d	5,300					

Table 12— Trial Balance of G. Nagle as on 31 March 1996.

Balances	DR	CR
Cash	1,530	
Bank	7,840	
Premises	50,000	
Motor Vehicles	20,000	
Stock	3,000	
Share Capital		79,660
Purchases	14,000	
Sales		18,100
Purchase Returns		2,000
Sales Returns	3,000	
Wages	800	
Advertising	400	
VAT		310
Creditors: J. Coffey		6,900
P. Lynch		2,300
Debtors: D. Mulcahy	3,400	
P. Morgan	5,300	
	109,270	109,270

Example and Questions Books of First Entry, Ledgers and Trial Balance

1.

Barton and Condon Ltd had the following balances in the company's accounts on 1 January 1990.

Cash €350, Bank €6,050, Stock €4,340, Motor Vans €6,800, Premises €40,000.

Debtors: T. Power €1,300, C. Keane €640, J. Shaw €380, J. Fletcher €180.

Total Assets figure = Total Liabilities

Creditors: J. Foran €750, M. Scanlon €690, D. Dunne €60, Share Capital €58,540.

(A) Enter these balances in the General Journal and post to the appropriate ledger accounts.

(B) Enter the following transactions in the books of Original Entry, post to the ledgers and extract a Trial Balance as at 31 January 1990.

Apply a VAT rate of 10% to all purchases, sales and returns.

01 Jan.	Cash Sales lodged €1,600.
02 Jan.	Received cheque from T. Power €900.
03 Jan.	Cash Sales lodged €2,400.
04 Jan.	Purchased goods on credit from M. Scanlon €1,500 (invoice no. 19).
04 Jan.	Paid Insurance by cheque €220.
07 Jan.	Cash Sales lodged €2,500.
08 Jan.	Paid wages by cheque €240.
08 Jan.	Sold goods on credit to C. Keane €300 (invoice. no. 48).
09 Jan.	Purchased goods on credit from J. Foran €7,300. (invoice. no. 691).
11 Jan.	Paid ESB by cheque €103.
14 Jan.	Cash Sales lodged €4,900.
15 Jan.	Sold goods on credit to T. Power €700 (invoice no. 49).
15 Jan.	Paid M. Scanlon €2,190 by cheque.
17 Jan.	Returned goods to J. Foran €700 (credit note no. 236) received.
18 Jan.	Bank charges €18.
19 Jan.	Purchased new van and paid by €8,200 cheque + VAT 20%.
20 Jan.	Purchased goods on credit from D. Dunne €300 (invoice no. 13).
21 Jan.	Returned goods to D. Dunne €100 (credit note no. 16).
22 Jan.	Paid D. Dunne €280 by cheque to clear his account.
23 Jan.	Purchased goods on credit from M. Scanlon €6,200 (invoice no. 25).
24 Jan.	Sold goods on credit to J. Shaw €2,000 (invoice no. 50).
24 Jan.	Cash Sales lodged €7,900.
25 Jan.	Cash Sales €460.
26 Jan.	Paid for postage stamps by cash €35.

2.

Foley and Keane Ltd had the following balance in the company's accounts on 1 February 1990.

Cash €620, Bank €3,820, Motor Vehicles €9,000, Equipment €6,500 Stock €23,000.

Debtors: C. Hannon €1,260. J. Sheehan €700 and K. Walsh €1,100.

Creditors: M. Boyle €1,400, P. Cummins €600,

Share Capital €44,000.

(A) Enter these balances in the General Journal and post to the relevant ledger accounts

(B) Record the following transactions in books of Original Entry, post to the ledgers and extract a Trial Balance as at 28 February 1990.

Apply VAT 10% on all purchases, sales and returns.

01 Feb.   Received €1,260 from C. Hannon by cheque.
02 Feb.   Cash Sales €400.
03 Feb.   Received from J. Sheehan Cash €200.
04 Feb.   Paid Insurance €250 by cheque.
05 Feb.   Sold goods on credit for K. Walsh for €5,000.
06 Feb.   Paid for repairs €120 by cash.
07 Feb.   K. Walsh returned goods €1,000 (credit note no. 5).
08 Feb.   Paid wages by cheque €800.
09 Feb.   Sold goods on credit to C. Hannon €8,000 (invoice no. 85).
10 Feb.   Paid rent by cheque €400.
11 Feb.   Cash Sales €1,200.
12 Feb.   Purchased goods on credit from P. Cummins €9,000 (invoice no. 48).
13 Feb.   Sold goods on credit €4,500 to J. Sheehan (invoice no. 86).
14 Feb.   J. Sheehan returned goods €500 (credit note no. 6).
15 Feb.   Returned goods to P. Cummins €500 (credit note no. 11).
16 Feb.   Paid advertising €80 by cash.
17 Feb.   Sold equipment on credit to P. Keating €1,000 (no VAT).
19 Feb.   Cash Sales lodged €980.
22 Feb.   Paid P. Cummins €7,000 by cheque on account.
26 Feb.   Paid wages by cheque €800.

3.

Cosgrave Ltd had the following balances in the company's accounts on 1 March 1990.

Premises €80,000, Motor Vehicles €35,000, Machinery €20,000, Fixtures and Fittings €5,000, Stock €2,300.

Debtors: P. Drummey €4,000, F. Leahy €2,500, S. Fennell €5,600, Cash €400, Bank €9,600.

Creditors: P. Hallahan €3,000, D. Healy €4,000, C. Connolly €8,000, Share Capital €149,400.

(A) Enter these balances in General Journal and post to the appropriate ledger accounts.

(B) Record the following transactions in the books of Original Entry, post to the ledgers and extract a Trial Balance as at 31 March 1990.
Apply VAT 10% on all purchases, sales and returns.

01 Mar.	Received a cheque from P. Drummey €400.
02 Mar.	Purchased goods on credit from P. Hallahan €5,000 (invoice no.191).
03 Mar.	Paid for repairs by cheque €500.
04 Mar.	Returned goods to P. Hallahan €500 (credit note no. 18).
05 Mar.	Cash Sales €250.
06 Mar.	Sold goods on credit to P. Drummey €10,000 (invoice no. 18).
08 Mar.	Sales Returns from P. Drummey €600 (credit note no. 3).
09 Mar.	Paid insurance by cheque €320.
10 Mar.	Paid for advertising €110 by cash.
11 Mar.	Received a cheque from P. Drummey €3,000.
12 Mar.	Sold goods on credit to F. Leahy €3,500 (invoice no. 19).
13 Mar.	Cash Sales €360.
15 Mar.	Paid wages by cheque €500.
16 Mar.	Cash Sales €480.
17 Mar.	Sold goods on credit to S. Fennell €8,000 (invoice no. 20).
20 Mar.	Paid ESB by cheque €207.
21 Mar.	Received a cheque €4,000 from S. Fennell.
23 Mar.	Purchased motor van €11,000 and paid by cheque (VAT 20%).
24 Mar.	Cash Sales €1,200 lodged.
25 Mar.	Purchased goods on credit from D. Healy €3,000 (invoice no. 50).
26 Mar.	Paid D. Healy €5,500 on account by cheque.

4.

Moran Ltd had the following balances in its accounts on 1 April 1990.

Premises €6,000, Delivery Vans €25,000, Machinery €40,000, Office Furniture and Equipment €8,000, Cash €220, Bank €7940, Stock €22,000. Debtors: K. Curran €4,300, D. Flynn €3,800, A. Moore €5,000. Creditors: K. Walsh €8,200, J. Barton €2,660, F. Leahy €1,200.

Share Capital €110,200.

(A) Enter the above balances in the General Journal and post to the relevant ledger accounts.

(B) Record the following transactions in the books of Original Entry, post to ledgers and extract a Trial Balance as at 30 April 1990.

VAT is 10% on sales purchases and returns.

01 Apr.	Cash Sales €420.
02 Apr.	Sold goods on credit to K. Curran €3,000 (invoice no. 8).
03 Apr.	Paid insurance by cheque €440.
04 Apr.	Paid wages by cheque €480.
05 Apr.	Sold goods on credit to K. Curran €3,000 (invoice no. 7).
06 Apr.	Cash Sales lodged €800.
07 Apr.	Paid repairs €80 by cash.
08 Apr.	Sales Returns €500 from K. Curran (credit note no. 4).
09 Apr.	Sold goods on credit to D. Flynn €4,000 (invoice no. 10).
10 Apr.	Purchased goods on credit from K. Walsh €6,000 (invoice no. 90).
11 Apr.	Cash Sales €600.
12 Apr.	Received cheque for €400 from K. Curran on account.
13 Apr.	Returned goods to K. Walsh €600 (credit note no. 18).
14 Apr.	Paid K. Walsh €11,000 by cheque on account.
15 Apr.	Cash Sales €300
16 Apr.	Sold goods on credit to K. Curran €3,500 (invoice no. 11).
17 Apr.	Paid wages €480 by cheque.
20 Apr.	Sold goods on credit to A. Moore €1,000 (invoice no. 12).
22 Apr.	Received a cheque from A. Moore to clear his account.
23 Apr.	Purchased goods on credit from J. Barton €10,000 (invoice no. 63).
24 Apr.	Paid F. Leahy by cheque to clear his account.
25 Apr.	Cash Sales lodged €800.

5.

A. O'Sullivan Ltd had the following balances in its account on 1 December 1990.
Premises €80,000, Machinery €10,000, Motor Vehicles €25,000, Office Equipment €6,000, Furniture and Fittings €8,000. Cash €300, Bank €13,210, Stock €9,700.
Debtors: M. Scanlon €4,800, K. Kiely €7,200, P. Stack €6,300. Creditors: G. Ashe €6,800, J. Browne €4,200, J. White €5,000.
Share Capital €154,510.

(A) Enter these balances in the General Journal and post to the relevant ledger accounts.

(B) Record the following in the books of Original Entry, post to the ledgers and extract a Trial Balance as at 31 December 1990. VAT is 10% on all sales, purchases and returns.

01 Dec. Cash Sales €160.
01 Dec. Paid rent €400 by cheque.
02 Dec. Sold goods on credit to M. Scanlon €3,200 (invoice no. 141).
03 Dec. Sold goods on credit to K. Kiely €3,600 (invoice no. 142).
04 Dec. Sales Returns €600 from M. Scanlon.
05 Dec. Cash Sales lodged €480.
05 Dec. Paid insurance €380 by cheque.
06 Dec. Purchased goods on credit from J. Brown €3,600 (invoice no.222).
07 Dec. Returned goods to J. Brown €800.
08 Dec. Received cheque €6,200 from M. Scanlon.
09 Dec. Purchased goods on credit from J. White €6,000 (invoice no. 63).
10 Dec. Purchased goods on credit from J. White €2,000 (invoice no. 64).
11 Dec. Cash Sales €240.
12 Dec. Returned goods to J. White €500.
13 Dec. Paid J. White €9,500 on account.
14 Dec. Purchased goods on credit from G. Ashe €3,200.
15 Dec. Paid G. Ashe €10,000 by cheque to clear his account.
16 Dec. Received a cheque €6,000 from P. Stack.
17 Dec. Sold goods on credit €4,000 to P. Stack (invoice no. 143).
18 Dec. Received a cheque from K. Kiely €8,000.
22 Dec. Cash Sales €200.
23 Dec. Paid salaries by cheque €1,800.
29 Dec. Sold goods on credit to J. Murphy €2,000 (invoice no. 144).

6.

(A) Enter the following balances of Quinlan Ltd in the General Journal and post to the relevant ledger accounts.

Land and buildings €75,000, Fixtures and Fittings €20,000, Machinery and Equipment €30,000, Stock €11,000, Bank Overdraft €8,450, Cash €30.

Debtors: D. Barnes €6,300, T. Galvin €7,800, M. Brett €6,600.

Creditors: B. Conway €4,950, K. Coffey, €6,780, C. Walsh €15,550. Issued Share Capital €121,000.

(B) Record the following transactions in the books of Original Entry, post to the ledgers and extract a Trial Balance as at 31 May 1991. VAT is 10% on all sales purchases and returns.

01 May	Cash Sales €540.
02 May	Paid wages €420 (cheque no. 91).
03 May	Sold goods on credit to D. Barnes €4,000 (invoice no. 91).
04 May	Received returns from D. Barnes €500 (credit note no. 17).
06 May	Paid insurance by cheque €330.
07 May	Purchased goods on credit from B. Conway for €4,000 (invoice no. 121).
08 May	Sold machine for €5,000 which was lodged to bank.
09 May	Paid wages €420 by cheque.
10 May	Returned goods to B. Conway €500.
12 May	Cash Sales lodged €2,000.
14 May	Sold goods on credit to D. Barnes €5,000 (invoice no. 92).
16 May	Received cheque €8,000 from D. Barnes.
16 May	Paid wages by cheque €420.
17 May	Sold goods on credit to T. Galvin €5,000 (invoice no. 93).
18 May	Purchased goods on credit from C. Walsh €11,000 (invoice no. 201).
20 May	Purchased goods on credit from K. Coffey €3,000. (invoice no. 641).
21 May	Sold goods on credit to M. Brett €2,000 (invoice no. 94).
22 May	Paid wages by cheque €420.
23 May	Received cheque €10,000 from T. Galvin.
24 May	Paid C. Walsh €26,550 by cheque.
25 May	Received cheque from M. Brett €7,000.

7.

(A) Record the following balances and entries in the books of Original Entry of M. Barnes Ltd, post to the ledgers and extract a Trial Balance as at 30 June 1991.

June 1: Premises €120,000 Motor Vehicles €70,000, Plant & Machinery €50,000, Office Equipment €20,000, Stock €24,000, Cash €150, Bank €8,850.

Debtors: J. Hayes €14,600, M. Sheridan €6,950, R. Casey €2,750.

Creditors: T. Murphy €8,900, A. Phelan €8,400.

Issued Share Capital €300,000.

Apply VAT 10% to all purchases, sales and returns.

01 June Sold goods on credit to J. Hayes €7,000 (invoice no. 502).

02 June Paid for repairs to motor vehicle by cash €70.

03 June Cash Sales lodged €2,400.

04 June Cash Sales €600.

05 June Sales Returns from J. Hayes €1,000.

06 June Received cheque from J. Hayes €20,600.

07 June Purchased goods on credit from T. Murphy €7,000 (invoice no. 1041).

08 June Paid light and heat by cheque €480.

09 June Returned goods to T. Murphy €500.

10 June Sold goods on credit to M. Sheridan €4,000. (invoice no. 502).

11 June Sold goods on credit to Sheridan €3,000 (invoice no. 503).

12 June Received cheque from M. Sheridan for €9,000.

14 June Cash Sales €350.

16 June Cash Sales lodged €400.

19 June Purchased goods on credit from A. Phelan €33,000.

20 June Paid A. Phelan €6,000 on account by cheque.

21 June Received cheque from R. Casey €2,750 to clear his account.

22 June Purchased goods on credit from C. Harty €4,000 (invoice no. 63).

24 June Cash Sales lodged €700.

26 June Cash Sales €600.

28 June Paid wages and salaries €1,200 by cheque.

8.

(A) Record the following balances and transactions in the books of Original Entry of Fitzgerald Ltd then post to the ledgers and extract a Trial Balance as at 30 November 1990.

Leasehold Premises €95,000 Fixtures and Fittings €20,000, Equipment €15,000, Stock €38,000, Cash €600, Bank Overdraft €2,700, Bank Loan €40,000.

Debtors: D. Kinsella €7,000, S. Roche €6,100, C. Keane €9,500.

Creditors: M. Hurley €9,300, S. Shanahan €8,200, T. Power €11,000.

Issued Share Capital €120,000.

Apply VAT 10% on all purchases sales and returns.

01 Nov.	Paid rent €2,000 by cheque.
02 Nov.	Sold goods on credit to D. Kinsella €15,000 (invoice no. 878).
03 Nov.	Cash Sales €800
04 Nov.	Received cheque €5,000 from S. Roche.
05 Nov.	Paid rates by cheque €7,000.
06 Nov.	Sold goods on credit to C. Keane €20,000 (invoice No 879).
07 Nov.	Received cheque from D. Kinsella €10,000.
08 Nov.	Paid insurance €180 cash.
09 Nov.	Paid for repairs €40 cash
10 Nov.	Purchased goods on credit from T. Power €8,000 (invoice no. 421).
12 Nov.	Returned goods to T. Power €2,000.
14 Nov.	Paid wages and salaries €570 by cheque.
15 Nov.	Purchased goods on credit from M. Hurley €10,000 (invoice no. 1021).
17 Nov.	Returned goods €1,500 to M. Hurley.
18 Nov.	Cash Sales lodged €4,000.
20 Nov.	Sold goods on credit to S. Roche €5,000 (invoice no. 880).
22 Nov.	Sales Returns €200 from S. Roche.
23 Nov.	Purchased goods on credit €4,000 from S. Shanahan (invoice no. 63).
24 Nov.	Paid T. Power €12,000 by cheque.
25 Nov.	Received a cheque €25,000 from C. Keane.
27 Nov.	Paid wages and salaries €570 by cheque.
28 Nov.	Paid M. Hurley €17,800 by cheque.
30 Nov.	Lodged all cash in bank except €150.

9.

Martin Murphy's business had the following assets and liabilities on 1 April 1996.
Land and Buildings €130,000, Equipment €25,000, Motor Vans €30,000, Stock €11,000, Cash €90, Bank €8,640.

Debtors: P. Collins €9,600, J. Buckley €7,200.

Creditors: G. O'Doherty €8,700, D. McGrath €6,900. Share Capital €205,930.

(A) Record these balances in the General Journal and post the balances to the relevant ledger accounts.

(B) Write up the following transactions in the books of Original Entry i.e. Sales Book, Purchases Book, Returns Books and Cash Books and post to the ledgers and prepare a Trial Balance as at 30 April 1996. VAT is 10% on purchases, sales and returns.

01 Apr.	Sold goods on credit to J. Buckley €7,000.
02 Apr.	Purchased goods on credit from G. O'Doherty €12,000.
04 Apr.	Cash Sales lodged €1,600.
05 Apr.	Cash Sales €800.
07 Apr.	Paid for stationery €20 in cash.
08 Apr.	Cash Purchases €400.
10 Apr.	Returned goods to G. O'Doherty €1,000
11 Apr.	Paid G. O'Doherty €7,000 by cheque.
12 Apr.	Sold goods on credit to P. Collins €18,000.
14 Apr.	Sales Returns €2,000 from P. Collins.
15 Apr.	Paid wages and salaries by cheque €3,200
15 Apr.	Received a cheque for €22,000 from P. Collins.
20 Apr.	Purchased goods on credit from D. McGrath €8,000.
22 Apr.	Paid D. McGrath €15,700 by cheque.

10.

S. O'Mahony's business had the following assets and liabilities on 1 May 1996.

Buildings €50,000, Stock €12,000, Delivery Vans €15,000, Equipment €14,000, Cash €360, Bank €6,800.

Debtors: E. Fitzpatrick €8,000, B. Power €7,840.

Creditors: J. Wall €9,000, R. Tobin €7,000.

Share Capital €98,000.

(A) Record these balances in the General Journal and post the balances to the relevant ledger accounts.

(B) Write up the following transactions in the books of Original Entry, post to the ledgers and prepare a Trial Balance as at 31 May 1996. VAT is 10% on purchases, sales and returns.

01 May	Paid insurance €600 by cheque.
03 May	Sold goods on credit to E. Fitzpatrick for €10,000.
05 May	Sales Returns from E. Fitzpatrick €2,000.
06 May	Purchased goods on credit from J. Wall €8,000.
07 May	Purchased goods on credit from R. Tobin €6,000.
08 May	Returned goods to R. Tobin €1,000.
09 May	Received a cheque for €10,000 from E. Fitzpatrick.
10 May	Cash Sales lodged €2,000.
12 May	Paid wages by cheque €700.
14 May	Sold goods on credit to B. Power €6,000.
15 May	Paid J. Wall €17,800 by cheque.
16 May	Cash Sales €400.
17 May	Paid R. Tobin €10,000 by cheque.

1.

The books of Barr Ltd showed the following balances on 1 May 1999.

Machinery €90,000.

Creditor: Keane Ltd €24,000.

(A) Enter these balances in the General Journal, find the Ordinary Share Capital balance and post these balances to the ledgers.

(B) Post the relevant figures from the Sales Book and Purchases Book below to the ledgers.

SALES DAY BOOK

Date	Details	Invoice No	F	Net	VAT	Total
06 May	Carey Ltd	26	DL7	48,000	6,000	54,000

PURCHASES DAY BOOK

Date	Details	Invoice No.	F			
08 May	Keane Ltd	48	CL14	20,000	2,500	22,500

(C) Record the following bank transactions from the month of May and post relevant figures to the ledger.

Note: Analyse the transactions using the following money column headings:

Debit (Receipts) Side: Bank, Sales, VAT, Debtors.

Credit (Payments) Side: Bank, Purchases, VAT, Creditors, Office Expenses.

03 May   Paid office expenses (cheque no. 19) €4,500.

08 May   Cash Sales lodged €45,000 (€40,000 + €5,000 VAT).

12 May   Purchases for resale €16,000 + 12.5% VAT (cheque no. 19).

14 May   Paid Keane Ltd €30,000 (cheque no. 20).

29 May   Carey Ltd paid its account in full which was lodged.

(D) Balance the accounts on 31 May 1999 and extract a Trial Balance as on that date.

2.

Murphy Ltd had the following balances in its General Journal on 1 January 1995.

GENERAL JOURNAL

Date	Details	F	DR	CR
01 Jan.	Bank	GL1	12,000	
	Debtor: J. Cooney Ltd	DL1	8,000	
	Ordinary Share Capital	GL2		20,000
			€20,000	€20,000

Being Assets, Liabilities and Share Capital of Murphy Ltd on 1 January 1996.

(A) Post the balances given in the General Journal to the relevant accounts.

(B) Post the relevant figures from the Sales Book and Sales Returns Book below to the ledgers.

SALES DAY BOOK

Date	Details	Invoice No.	F	Net	VAT	Total
05 Jan.	J. Cooney Ltd	80	DL1	8,000	1,000	9,000
07 Jan.	S. Keane Ltd	81	DL2	24,000	3,000	27,000
				€32,000	€4,000	€36,000
				GL3	GL4	

SALES RETURNS BOOK

Date	Details	Cr. Note No.	F	Net	VAT	Total
18 Jan. 1996	S. Keane Ltd	5	DL2	4,000	500	4,500
				GL5	GL4	

(C) Record the following bank transactions for the month of May 1995. Post the relevant figures to the ledger.

Note: Analyse the bank transactions using the following money column headings:
Debit (Receipts) Side: Bank, Sales, Vat, Debtors, Ordinary Share Capital.
Credit (Payments) Side: Bank, Purchased, VAT, Insurance.

03 May   Cash Sales lodged €38,250 (€34,000 + €4,250 VAT).
07 May   Purchases for resale (cheque no. 17) €16,800 + 12.5% VAT.
13 May   Paid insurance (cheque no. 18) €3,200.
18 May   J. Cooney Ltd paid his account in full (receipt no. 48).
28 May   Murphy Ltd shareholders invested €40.000 and this was lodged.

(D) Balance the accounts on 31 January 1995 and extract a Trial Balance as at that date.

3.

The books of M. Kiely Ltd showed the following balances on 1 February 1995

	€
Motor Vehicles	18,200
Bank Overdraft	2,600
Debtor C. Hayes	5,200

(A) Enter these balances in the General Journal, find the Ordinary Share Capital balances, and post these balances to the ledgers.

(B) Post the relevant figures from the Purchases Book and Purchases Returns Book below to the ledgers.

PURCHASES BOOK

Date	Details	Invoice No.	F	Net	VAT	Total
02 Feb.	Mulcahy Ltd	116	CL7	6,400	800	7,200
13 Feb.	Fitzgerald Ltd	88	CL8	6,400	2,050	18,450
				€12,800	€2,850	€15,650

PURCHASES RETURNS BOOK

Date	Details	Cr. Note No.	F	Net	VAT	Total
16 May	Fitzgerald Ltd	48	CL8	4,880	610	5,490
				4,880	610	5,490

(C) Write up the following bank transactions and post the relevant figures to the ledgers. Analyse the bank transactions under the following money column headings:

Debit (Receipts) Side: Bank, Sales, VAT, Debtors.

Credit (Payments) Side: Bank, Purchases, VAT, Creditors, other.

03 Feb. Paid insurance (cheque no. 1) €1,600.

05 Feb. Cash Sales lodged €36,225 (€32,200 + €4,025 VAT).

10 Feb. Purchased motor van (cheque no. 2) €16,000.

12 Feb. Paid Mulcahy Ltd (cheque no. 3) €7,200.

14 Feb. Purchases for Resale (cheque no. 4) €7,000 + 12.5% VAT.

27 Feb. C. Hayes paid €4,000 by cheque which was lodged.

(D) Balance the accounts on 28 February 1995 and extract a Trial Balance as at that date.

4.

Kennedy Ltd had the following balances in its General Journal on 1 March 1995.

GENERAL JOURNAL

Date	Details	F	DR	CR
01 March	Motor Vehicles	GL1	25,000	
	Premises		80,000	
	Plant & Machinery		10,000	
	Bank		2,000	
	Debtor: R. Johnson Ltd		6,000	
	Creditor: J. Cooney Ltd			33,000
	Ordinary Share Capital			90,000
			€123,000	€123,000

The following transactions took place during the month of March 1995.

Credit Transactions

03 Mar. Purchased goods for resale on credit from J. Cooney Ltd (invoice no. 401) €30,000 + 15% VAT.

12 Mar. Sold goods on credit to Morrissey Ltd (invoice no. 242) €6,000 + 15% VAT.

21 Mar. Sold goods on credit to Johnson Ltd (invoice no. 243) €20,000 + 15% VAT.

Bank Transactions

04 Mar. 1995 Paid insurance (cheque no. 61) €600.

07 Mar. 1995 Cash Sales lodged €9,200 (includes VAT €1,200).

17 Mar. 1995 Purchased goods for resale (cheque no. 62) €1,500 + VAT 15%.

24 Mar. 1995 R. Johnson Ltd settled their account in full by cheque and this was lodged.

29 Apr. 1995 Paid J. Cooney Ltd (cheque no. 63) €32,000.

(A) Post the balances as at 1 March to the relevant accounts.

(B) Record the transactions for the month of May in the appropriate books of First Entry and post the relevant figures to the ledger.
Note: Analyse the bank transactions using the following money column headings:
Debit (Receipts) Side: Bank, Sales, VAT, Debtors.
Credit (Payments) Side: Bank, Purchases, VAT, Creditors, Insurance.

(C) Balance the accounts on 31 March 1995 and extract a Trial Balance on that date.

5.

The following Trial Balance was extracted from the books of Cummins Ltd at the 31 March 1995.

	€DR	€CR
Creditor: E. Sheehan		40,000
Premises	80,000	
Equipment	10,000	
Motor Vans	20,000	
Bank	5,000	
Issued Capital — 75,000		
@ €1 each		75,000

Credit Transactions for the month of April were recorded in the books as follows.

PURCHASES BOOK

Date	Details	Invoice No.	F	Net	VAT	Total
05 Apr.	E. Sheehan	181	CL4	10,000	1,000	11,000
22 Apr.	E. Sheehan	199	CL4	18,000	1,800	19,800
				€28,000	€2,800	€30,800

PURCHASES RETURNS BOOK

Date	Details	Cr. Note No.	F	Net	VAT	Total
08 Apr.	E. Sheehan	28	CL4	1,500	150	1,650
				1,500	150	1,650

The following bank transactions took place during the month ended 30 April 1995.

02 Apr.   Purchases for Resale (cheque no. 863) €35,000 + VAT at 10%.
04 Apr.   Cash Sales lodged (receipt no. 94) €125,000 + VAT at 10%.
07 Apr.   Paid wages (cheque no. 864) €1,500.
14 Apr.   Purchase of equipment (cheque no. 865) €23,000.
16 Apr.   Paid insurance by (cheque no. 866) €2,600.
21 Apr.   Paid E. Sheehan by (cheque no. 867) €60,000.

The closing stock of goods on 30 April 1995 was valued at €15,000.

(A) Enter the above Trial Balance figures into relevant accounts.

(B) Post the relevant figures from the Purchases and Purchases Returns Books to the ledger.

(C) Write up the bank transactions under the following headings:
Debit Side: Sales, Other, VAT, Bank.
Credit Side: Purchases, Other, VAT, Bank, and post the relevant figures to the ledger.

(D) Balance the accounts and extract a Trial Balance as at 30 April 1995.

(E) Prepare Trading and Profit and Loss for month ended 30 April 1995.

6.

J. Lynch Ltd a private limited company was formed on 1 May 1995. The shareholders invested €50,000 for 50,000 €1 shares and this was lodged to the company bank account.

The following transactions took place during the month of May 1995.

Credit Transactions

03 May Purchased goods on credit from Connery Ltd (invoice no 65) €14,000 + 21% VAT.

09 May Purchased goods on credit from Kiely Ltd (invoice no. 174 €5,800 + Vat 21%.

11 May. Returned goods to Connery Ltd (credit note no. 16 €1,400 + VAT 21%).

Bank Transactions

02 May   Purchases for Resale (cheque no. 1) €10,000 + VAT 21%.

03 May   Paid insurance (cheque no. 2) €2,500.

04 May   Purchased motor van (cheque no. 3) €15,000.

14 May 1995   Cash Sales lodged €14,520 (€12,000 + €2,520 VAT).

27 May 1995   Paid Connery Ltd their account in full (cheque no. 4).

(A) Enter the transaction of 1 May 1995 into the appropriate ledger accounts.

(B) Record the transactions for month of May in the appropriate books of First Entry and post relevant figures to the ledger.
Note: Analyse the bank transactions using the following money column headings:
Debit (Receipts) Side: Bank, Sales, VAT, Other.
Credit (Payments) Side: Bank, Purchases, VAT, Creditors, Other.

(C) Balance the accounts on the 31 May 1995 and extract a Trial Balance as on that date.

7.

S. Walsh Ltd a private limited company was formed on 1 June 1995 the share-holders invested €80,000 and this was lodged to the company bank account.

The following transactions occurred during the month of June 1995.

Credit Transactions

02 June Purchased goods on credit from Lonergan Ltd (invoice no. 64) €14,000 + VAT 21%.

03 June Purchased goods on credit from Kelly Ltd (invoice no. 297) €28,000 + VAT 21%.

05 June Sold goods on credit to Moore Ltd (invoice no. 1) €34,000 + VAT 21%.

07 June Sales Returns from Moore Ltd (credit note no. 1) €8,000 + VAT 21%.

11 June Sold goods on credit to Ryan Ltd (invoice no. 2) €1,200 + VAT 21%.

Bank Transactions

01 June Sale of €80,000 €1 shares lodged.

03 June Purchased Premises (cheque no. 1) €60,000.

05 June Paid expenses (cheque no. 2) €3,200.

07 June Cash Sales lodged €16,940 (€14,000 + €2,940 VAT).

14 June Purchases for Resale (cheque no. 3) €9,000 + 21% VAT.

16 June Received cheque for €20,000 from Moore Ltd on account which was lodged.

22 June Paid Lonergan Ltd account in full (cheque no. 4).

(A) Enter the transaction of 1 June 1995 into the appropriate ledger account.

(B) Record the transactions for the month of June in the appropriate books of First Entry and post the relevant figures to the ledger.

Note: Analyse the bank transactions using the following money column headings:

Debit (Receipts) Side: Bank, Sales, VAT, Other.

Credit (Payments) Side: Bank, Purchases, VAT, Creditors, other.

(C) Balance the accounts on 30 June 1995 and extract a Trial Balance as on that date.

8.

The following Trial Balance was extracted from the books of Hickey Ltd, a retail shop, on 1 July 1995. It has an Authorised Share Capital of €80,000.

Bank	22,000	
Reserves		8,000
Fixed Assets	40,000	
Stock at 1 July	6,000	
Debtor: D. Coffey		14,000
Creditor: S. Dempsey		14,000
Issued Shares:50,000		
@€1		50,000
	€72,000	€72,000

Credit transactions for the month of July were:

03 July   Purchases from S. Dempsey (invoice no. 4876) €6,000 + VAT 10%.
08 July   Purchases from S. Dempsey (invoice no. 4899) €1,000 + VAT 10%.
09 July   Returned goods to S. Dempsey (credit note no. 516) €600 + VAT 10%.
11 July   Sold goods on credit to D. Coffey (invoice no. 606) 7000 + VAT 10%.
12 July   Had Sale Returns from D. Coffey (credit note no.) 99 €2,000 + VAT 10%.

The following bank transactions took place during the month of July:

02 July   Paid for goods for resale €4,800 + 10% VAT (cheque no. 161).
04 July   Paid for new Office Equipment €4,000 (cheque no. 162).
06 July   Paid S. Dempsey €12,000 (cheque no. 163).
08 July   Cash Sales lodged €14,000 + 10% VAT (receipt no. 7841).
11 July   Paid wages €940 (cheque no.163).
16 July   Received cheque from D. Coffey to clear his account.
23 July   Paid insurance €2,060 (cheque no. 164).
Closing stock of goods 31 July 1995 €12,000.

(A) Enter the above Trial Balance figures into relevant accounts.
(B) Write up the books of First Entry for the month ended 31 June 1995 and post the relevant figures to the ledger.
(C) Balance the accounts at 31 July 1995.
(D) Extract a Trial Balance as at 31 July 1995.
(E) Prepare final accounts for the month ended 31 July 1995 (Trading and Profit and Loss Account) and a Balance Sheet as at date.

9.

P. O'Connor Ltd had the following balances in its General Journal on 1 August 1995.

GENERAL JOURNAL

Date	Details	F	DR	CR
01 Aug.	Debtor: T. O'Donnell Ltd	DL1	7,000	
	Bank	CB	23,000	
	Ordinary Share Capital	GL1		30,000
	Assets, Liabilities and Share			
	Capital on 1 August 1995		€30,000	€30,000

(A) Post the balances given in the General Journal to the relevant accounts.

(B) Post the relevant figures from the Sales Book and Sales Returns Book below to the ledgers.

SALES DAY BOOK

Date	Details	Invoice No.	F	Net	VAT	Total
12 Aug.	T. O'Donnell Ltd	649	DL1	8,000	1,680	9,680
14 Aug.	B. Meehan Ltd	650	DL2	25,000	5,250	30,250
				€33,000	€6,930	€39,930
				GL2	GL3	

SALES RETURNS DAY BOOK

Date	Details	Cr. Note No.	F	Net	VAT	Total
15 Aug.	B. Meehan Ltd	14		6,000	1,260	7,260
				GL4	GL3	

(C) Record the following bank transactions for the month of August and post relevant figures to the ledger.
Note: Analyse the bank transactions using the following money column headings:
Debit (Receipts) Side: Bank, Sales, VAT, Debtor, Ordinary Share Capital.
Credit (Payments) Side: Bank Purchases, VAT, General Expenses.

Bank Transactions
02 Aug. Purchases for resale (cheque no. 78) €26,000 + VAT 21%.
03 Aug. Paid General Expenses (cheque no. 79) €1,000.
08 Aug. Cash Sales lodged €41,140 (€34,000 + €7,140 VAT).
14 Aug. T. O'Donnell Ltd paid its account in full (receipt no. 63).
15 Aug. B. Meehan Ltd paid €15,000 on account (receipt no. 99).
27 Aug. T. O'Donnell Ltd shareholders invested €40,000 in company shares and this was lodged.

(D) Balance the accounts on 31 August 1995 and extract a Trial Balance as at that date.

10.

B. Flynn Ltd, a private limited company, was formed on 1 September 1995. The shareholders invested €80,000 (80,000 €1 shares) and this was lodged to the company bank account.

The following transactions took place during the month of September 1995.

Credit Transactions

03 Sept. Purchased goods on credit from Tobin Ltd (invoice no. 48) €11,000 + VAT 12%.

05 Sept. Purchased goods on credit from Stack Ltd (invoice no. 8) €9,400 + VAT 12%.

07 Sept. Returned goods to Tobin Ltd (credit note no. 29) €2,400 + VAT 12%.

12 Sept. Sold goods on credit to Moore Ltd (invoice no. 1) €15,000 + VAT 12%.

14 Sept. Sales Returns from Moore Ltd (credit note no. 1) €3,000 + VAT 12%.

Bank Transactions

02 Sept. Purchased buildings (cheque no. 1) €50,000.

03 Sept. Purchased motor vehicle (cheque no. 2) €15,000.

05 Sept. Purchases for resale (cheque no. 3) €7,000 + VAT 12%.

06 Sept. Paid insurance (cheque no. 4) €1,500.

09 Sept. Cash Sales lodged €20,160 (€18,000 + €2,160 VAT).

26 Sept. Paid Tobin Ltd their account in full (cheque no. 5).

27 Sept. Received cheque €7,000 from Moore Ltd on account.

(A) Enter the transaction of 1 September 1995 in the appropriate ledger accounts.

(B) Record the transactions for the month of September in the appropriate books of First Entry and post the relevant figures to the ledger.
Note: Analyse the bank transactions using the following money column headings:
Debit (Receipts) Side: Bank, Sales, VAT, Other.
Credit (Payments) Side: Bank, Purchases, Vat, Creditors, Other.

(C) Balance the accounts on 30 September 1995 and extract a Trial Balance as on that date.

11.

The books of A. Murray Ltd showed the following balances on 1 October 1995.

Debtor: P. Casey Ltd	5,200
Premises	60,000
Creditor: B. Barry Ltd	6,000
Bank	800

(A) Enter these balances in the General Journal, find the Ordinary Share Capital balance and post these balances to the ledgers.

(B) Post the relevant figures from the Purchases Book and Purchases Returns Book below to the ledgers.

PURCHASES BOOK

Date	Details	Invoice No.	F	Net	VAT	Total
9 Oct.	B. Barry Ltd	14	CL1	8,800	1,100	9,900
14 Oct.	A. Brennan Ltd	63	CL2	12,000	1,500	13,500
			GL2	€20,800	€2,600	€23,400

PURCHASES RETURNS BOOK

Date	Details	Cr. Note No.	F	Net	VAT	Total
16 Oct.	A. Brennan Ltd	17	CL2	2,000	250	2,250
			GL3	€2,000	€250	€2,250

(C) Write up the following bank transactions and post relevant figures to the ledgers, analysing the bank transactions under the following money column headings:
Debit (Receipts) Side: Bank, Sales, VAT, Debtors.
Credit (Payments) Side: Bank, Purchases, VAT, Creditors, Other.

03 Oct.   P. Casey Ltd paid €4,000 by cheque which was lodged.
07 Oct.   Cash Sales lodged €31,500 (€28,000 + €3,500 VAT).
09 Oct.   Purchased office equipment (cheque no. 117) €8,000.
13 Oct.   Paid R. Barry Ltd €7,700 (cheque no. 118).
14 Oct.   Purchases for resale (cheque no. 119) €6,000 + 12.5% VAT.
16 Oct.   Paid general expenses (cheque no. 120) €1,400.

(D) Balance the accounts on 31 October 1995, and extract a Trial Balance as at that date.

12.

The books of Hegarty Ltd showed the following balances on 1 June 1997.
Premises €160,000.
Creditors: P. O'Connor Ltd €13,200.

(A) Enter these balances in the General Journal, find the Ordinary Share Capital balance, and post these balances to the ledgers.

(B) Post the relevant figures from the Purchases Book and Sales Book below to the ledgers.

PURCHASES BOOK

Date	Details	Invoice No.	F	Net	VAT	Total
05 June	P. O'Connor Ltd	73	CL3	22,000	4,620	26,620

SALES DAY BOOK

Date	Details	Invoice No.	F	Net	VAT	Total
07 June	M. McGinn Ltd	28	DL5	14,000	2,940	16,940

(C) Record the following bank transactions for the month of June and post the relevant figures to the ledger.

Note: Analyse the transactions using the following money column headings:
Debit (Receipts) Side: Bank, Sales, VAT, Debtors.
Credit (Payments) Side: Bank, Purchases, VAT, Creditors, Repairs.

02 June	Paid Repairs (cheque no. 1) €3,100.
04 June	Cash Sales lodged €41,140 (€34,000 + 7,140 VAT).
08 June 1997	Paid P. O'Connor Ltd (cheque no. 2) €24,200.
18 June 1997	Purchases for resale (cheque no. 3) €18,000 + 21% VAT.
27 June 1997	M. McGinn Ltd paid its account in full and it was lodged (receipt no. 48).

(D) Balance the accounts on 30 June 1997, and extract a Trial Balance as on that date.

13.

The following transactions took place during the month of June 1998.

Credit Transactions

01 June Purchased goods on credit from Spice Ltd (invoice no. 60) €20,000 + VAT 12.5%.

08 June Sold goods on credit to Pro Ltd (invoice no. 4) €32,000 + VAT 12.5%.

11 June Purchased goods on credit Cap Ltd (invoice no. 98) €16,000 + VAT 12.5%.

Bank Transactions

03 June Purchases for Resale (cheque no. 98) €10,000 + VAT 12.5%.

04 June Paid expenses (cheque no. 99) €2,400.

07 June Shareholders invest €50,000 and this was lodged.

08 June Paid Spice Ltd its account in full (cheque no. 100).

12 June Pro Ltd paid €24,000 and this was lodged (receipt no. 5).

(A) Record the transactions for the month of June 1998 in the appropriate books of First Entry, and post relevant figures to the ledger.
Note: Analyse the bank transactions using the following money column headings:
Debit (Receipts) Side: Bank, Share Capital, Debtors.
Credit (Payments) Side: Bank, Purchases, VAT, Creditors, Expenses.

(B) Balance the accounts on 30 June 1998 and extract a Trial Balance as on that date.

14.

The books of Dean Ltd showed the following balances on 1 May 2000.

Machinery €75,000.

Creditor: Brown Ltd €32,000.

(A) Enter these balances in the General Journal, find the Ordinary Share Capital balance and post these balances to the ledgers.

(B) Post the relevant figures from the Sales Book and Purchase Book below to the ledgers.

SALES DAY BOOK

Date	Details	Invoice No.	F	Net	VAT	Total
03 May	Houlihan Ltd	16	DL6	48,000	6,000	54,000

PURCHASES DAY BOOK

Date	Details	Invoice No.	F	Net	VAT	Total
06 May	Brown Ltd	25	CL4	32,000	4,000	36,000

(C) Record the following bank transactions for the month of May and post the relevant figures to the ledger.

Note: Analyse the transactions using the following money column headings:

Debit (Receipts) Side: Bank, Sales, VAT, Debtors.

Credit (Payments) Side: Bank, Purchases, VAT, Creditors, Insurance.

Bank Transactions

03 May	Cash Sales lodged €45,000 (€40,000 + €5,000 VAT).
05 May	Purchases for Resale (cheque no. 22) €24,000 + 12.5% VAT.
08 May	Paid Brown Ltd (cheque no. 23) €60,000.
10 May	Houlihan Ltd paid its account in full which was lodged (receipt no. 48).
22 May 1999	Paid rates €4,000 (cheque no. 24).

(D) Balance the accounts on 31 May 1999 and extract a Trial Balance as on that date.

Chapter 2
The Final Accounts

The final accounts are prepared at the end of the business year to show the annual Profit/Loss made by the business. They are made up of four sections:

Trading Account.
Profit and Loss Account.
Appropriation Account.
Balance Sheet.

The entries for the Final Accounts will come from the business's Trial Balance.

2.1 Trading Account

The Trading Account shows the **Gross Profit** or **Gross Loss** made by a business i.e. it shows the difference between the price paid for the goods purchased (Purchases) and the price obtained for the goods when sold (Sales).

A continuous combined Trading and Profit and Loss Account for the year ended is the usual format in the final accounts i.e. after calculating the Gross Profit in the Trading Account, the Profit and Loss Account can be proceeded with in continuation.

Example

Table 14 — Trading Account for J. Wood Ltd year ending 31 December 1996.

TRADING ACCOUNT FOR J. WOOD LTD YEAR ENDING 31 DECEMBER 1996

		€	€	€
	Sales			220,000
Less	Sales Returns			5,000
				215,000
Less	Cost of Sales			
	Opening Stock		30,000	
	Purchases	130,000		
Less	Purchases Returns	20,000	110,000	Minus
	Carriage Inwards		2,000	
	Customs Duty		11,000	
	Goods Available for Sale		153,000	
Less	Closing Stock		45,000	
	Cost of Sales			108,000
	Gross Profit			107,000

Note: The heading on the Trading Account is very important.

IMPORTANT TERMS AND DEFINITIONS

Net Sales
Net Sales = Sales – Sales Returns

Gross Profit
Gross Profit = Net Sales – Cost of Sales

Gross Loss
If Cost of Sales is greater than Net Sales a Gross Loss will be made by the business.

Returns Inwards
Also known as Sales Returns.

Returns Outwards
Also known as Purchases Returns.

Customs Duty
Also known as Import Duty or Duty on Purchases.

Carriage Inwards
Also known as Duty on Purchases.

2.2 Profit and Loss Account

The Profit and Loss Account will show the Gross Profit plus any additional income made by the business less the running expenses of the business, which will result in the **Net Profit**.

If the Net Profit is adequate, the shareholders may be paid a **Dividend**. This is subtracted from Net Profit.

GAINS

Items of extra income in addition to Gross Profit are referred to as Gains e.g. interest earned on money in the bank (Interest Received).

EXPENSES

These are the day-to-day running costs of a business and include adjustments and the depreciation of Fixed Assets.

Table 15 — Profit and Loss Account of J. Wood Ltd for the year ended 31 December 1996

PROFIT AND LOSS ACCOUNT OF J. WOOD LTD YEAR ENDED 31 DECEMBER 1996

		€	€	€
	Gross Profit			107,000
G	Rent Received		18,000	
A	Less Rent Received (Prepaid)		1,000	17,000
I	Interest Received		6,000	
N	Plus Interest Receivable Due		2,000	8,000
S	Commission Received			5,000
	Bad Debts Recovered			
	Discount Received			2,000
				139,000
	Less Cost Of Selling			
	Insurance	7,500		
	Less Insurance (Prepaid)	1,300	7,200	
	Advertising	4,000		
E	Advertising Due	2,000	6,000	
X	Postage and Stationery	900		
P	Less Stock of Stationery on Hand	100	800	
E	Carriage Outwards		4,000	
N	Bank Charges		300	
S	Interest on Bank Overdraft		200	
E	Bad Debts		400	
S	Light and Heat	8,000		
	Less Stock of Heating Oil on Hand	500	7,500	
	Rates		12,000	
	Depreciation: Motor Vans 15%	12,000		
	Office Equipment 10%	400		
	Plant Machinery 12%	12,000	24,400	
	Total Cost of Selling (Expenses)			62,800
	Net Profit			76,200
	Profit/Loss Account Balance (CR) Reserves			24,000
				100,200
	Less Dividends 8%			16,000
	Reserves Profit and Loss Account Balance			
	31 Dec. 1996			84,200

ADJUSTMENTS

1.   ITEMS PAID IN ADVANCE

These are items for the currrent business year that remain to be paid e.g. Advertising. They must be added to the expenses.

2.   DEPRECIATION

The loss in value of Fixed Assets due to wear and tear is termed depreciation. It is calculated as an expense in the Profit and Loss Account.

3.   ITEMS PAID IN ADVANCE

Money paid towards a particular expense such as Insurance or Stocks of Stationery may cover several months in the current business year. Their cost must therefore be subtracted from the relevant expense in the Profit and Loss Account.

2.3 Appropriation Account

The Appropriation Account shows the Net Profit plus any Profit (Reserves) left over (accumulated) from previous years less Dividends paid to the Shareholders.

2.4 Balance Sheet

The Balance Sheet is a list of a business's assets and liabilities on a particular date.
   The Balance Sheet is divided into four sections:

1. **Fixed Assets.**
2. **Current Assets.**
3. **Current Liabilities.**
4. **Financed By.**

ASSETS

Fixed Assets

These are permanent assets that remain in the business for a number of years e.g.
   Buildings
   Motor Vans
   Fixture and Fittings
   Machinery
   Office Equipment

Current Assets

These are assets that change from day-to-day in a business e.g.
    Stock
    Cash
    Debtors (customers who owe money to the business from credit sales)
    Bank (money in a bank account)
    Expenses Paid in Advance (prepaid)
    Gains Due to be Received
    Petty Cash (small amount of cash specially set aside to cover very small items of expenditure)

Liabilities
Current Liabilities

    Current Liabilities are owned by the business in the short term
    e.g. Creditors (arising from credit purchases)
    Bank Overdraft
    Expenses Due
    Gains Received (paid too soon or in advance)

Working Capital

Working Capital is calculated by subtracting current liabilities from current assets.

Net Assets

Net Assets are the total of fixed assets plus working capital.
These assets are usually **Financed By**:

 (i) Share Capital — Every company has an Authorised Share Capital i.e. a number of shares it is allowed to issue. Issued Share Capital is the amount of shares actually issued.
 (ii) Profit (Revenue) Reserves
(iii) Bank Loan

Worked Example

The following Trial Balance was extracted from the books of Capital Ltd on 31 December 1996. The Authorised Share Capital is 250,000 €1 Ordinary Shares.
  Prepare the company's Trading, Profit and Loss and Appropriation Accounts for the year ended 31 December 1996 and a Balance Sheet as at that date.

	DR €	CR €
Purchases and Sales	99,000	187,400
Returns	400	3,000
Issued Share Capital		200,000
Buildings	150,000	
Plant and Machinery	60,000	
Repairs	2,200	
Advertising	1,600	
Carriage In	2,400	
Customs Duty	4,450	
Motor Vehicles	40,000	
Office Equipment	6,000	
Furniture and Fittings	10,000	
Interest Receivable		2,600
Rates	3,000	
Rent Receivable		4,000
Bad Debts	250	
Commission	6000	
Wages and Salaries	22,000	
Postage and Stationery	800	
Telephone	2,200	
Opening Stock 01 Jan.1996	14,000	
Bank		1,400
Bank Deposit Account	43,600	
Debtors and Creditors	28,000	31,000
Bills (Payable) and Bills (Receivable)	2,000	3,000
Reserves (Profit Loss Balance)		65,500
	497,900	497,900

You are given the following information as at 31 December 1996:

  (i) Closing Stock €26,000
 (ii) Advertising Prepaid €400
(iii) Carriage Inwards Due €600
 (iv) Stock of Stationery on Hand €150
  (v) Interest Receivable Due €400
 (vi) Rent Received (Paid in Advance) €500
(vii) Depreciation: Plant and Machinery 10%, Motor Vehicles 15%, Office
     Equipment 10%, Furniture and Fittings 5%
(viii) Dividends Declared 12%

Table 16 — Trading, Profit and Loss and Appropriation Account of Capital Ltd year ending 31 December 1996

TRADING, PROFIT AND LOSS AND APPROPRIATION ACCOUNT OF CAPITAL LTD
YEAR ENDING 31 DECEMBER 1996

		€	€	€
	Sales			187,400
Less	Sales Returns			400
				187,000
LESS	**COST OF SALES**			
	Opening Stock		14,000	
	Purchases	99,000		
Less	Purchases Returns	3,000	96,000	
	Carriage Inwards	2,400		Subtract
Add	Carriage Inwards Due	600	3,000	
	Customs Duty		4,450	
	GOODS AVAILABLE FOR SALE		117,450	
Less	Closing Stock		26,000	
	COST OF SALES			91,450
	GROSS PROFIT			95,550
	Interest Receivable		2,600	
Add	Interest Receivable Due		400	3,000
	Rent Receivable		4,000	
Less	Rent Receivable (paid in advance)		500	3,500
				102,050
LESS	**COST OF SELLING**			
	Repairs		2,200	
	Advertising	1,600		
Less	Advertising (prepaid)	400	1,200	
	Rates		3,000	
	Bad Debts		250	
	Commission		6,000	
	Wages and Salaries		22,000	
	Postage and Stationery	800		
Less	Stock of Stationery on Hand	150	650	
	Telephone		2,200	
	Depreciation: Plant and Machinery 10%	6,000		
	Motor Vehicles 15%	6,000		
	Office Equipment 10%	600		
	Furniture and Fittings 5%	500	13,100	
Total Expenses				50,600
Net Profit				51,450
Profit and Loss 01 Jan. 1996				65,500
				116,950
Less	Dividends 12%			24,000
Profit and Loss Appropriation Account				
31 Dec. 1999				92,950

Table 17 — Balance Sheet of Capital Ltd as at 31 December 1996

BALANCE SHEET OF CAPITAL LTD AS AT 31 DECEMBER 1996

	Cost	Depreciation to Date	Net Book Value
	€	€	€
FIXED ASSETS			
Buildings	150,000		150,000
Plant and Machinery	60,000	6,000	54,000
Motor Vehicles	40,000	6,000	34,000
Office Equipment	6,000	600	5,400
Furniture and Fittings	10,000	500	9,500
	266,000	13,100	252,900
CURRENT ASSETS			
Bank Deposit Account		43,600	
Debtors		28,000	
Bills Receivable		2,000	
Closing Stock		26,000	
Advertising (Prepaid)		400	
Stock of Stationery on Hand		150	
Interest Receivable Due		400	
		100,550	
LESS CURRENT LIABILITIES			
Bank Overdraft (CR)	1,400		
Creditors	31,000		
Bills Payable	3,000		add
Carriage Inwards Due	600		
Rent Received (Paid in Advance)	500		
Dividends Due 12%	24,000	60,500	
Working Capital			40,050
Net Assets			292,950
Financed by:		Authorised	Issued
Share Capital €1 Ordinary Shares		250,000	200,000
RESERVES			
Profit and Loss Account 31 Dec. 1996			92,950
CAPITAL EMPLOYED			292,950

Notes

1. Dividends

If dividends are shown in additional information they have not yet been paid and must be deducted from profits in the Profit and Loss Appropriation Account and from Current Liabilities on the Balance Sheet.

If dividends are shown in the Trial Balance they have already been paid. In this case they must be deducted from profits in the Profit and Loss Appropriation Account only. Note that it is not necessary to include such dividends in Current Liabilities as they have already been paid.

2. *Trial Balance*

The Trial Balance is made up of two columns – a Debit Column (DR) and a Credit Column (CR). The debit column contains Assets and Expenses and the credit column contains Liabilities and Gains.

Notes on Trial Balance

Purchases and Sales	DR Purchases	CR Sales
	Purchases Sales Returns	Sales Purchases Returns
Bank CR so Current Liability (Bank Overdraft)		4,000
If DR a Current Asset (Bank)		
Rent if CR then Rent Received		3,000
Interest if CR then Interest Received		2,000
Rent DR then Rent paid	6,000	
VAT CR Current Liability		
VAT Dr Current Asset		

1. The figure for sales is on **CR** column. Purchases on **DR** column. Sometimes only one Returns Figure may be given in Trial Balance and the question may not state whether it is Purchases or Sales Returns. Sales Returns will be opposite to Sales in Trial Balance i.e. **DR** column shown by arrow above.
2. If Rent/Interest are included on **CR** column then they are Rent Received/Interest Received. If on **DR** column then they are expenses.
3. If VAT is on **CR** column in Trial Balance then it is a Current Liability. If on **DR** column then it is a Current Asset.

Practice Questions

Trading Account

In each of the following questions prepare a Trading Account for the year ended 31 December 1988.

1.

Opening Stock	€2,500
Sales	€23,000
Purchases	€14,200
Closing Stock	€1,900

2.

Opening Stock	€2,700
Sales	€24,600
Purchases	€13,500
Purchases Returns	€200
Sales Returns	€450
Closing Stock	€3,100

3.

Opening Stock	€4,600
Sales	€48,260
Sales Returns	€4,040
Purchases Returns	€290
Carriage Inwards	€360
Closing Stock	€2,900
Purchases	€29,060

4.

Opening Stock	€2,040
Purchases	€19,180
Import Duty	€260
Closing Stock	€2,490
Returns Outwards	€200
Sales	€48,230
Returns Inwards	€1,900
Closing Stock	€3,100

5.

Opening Stock	€4,200
Purchases	€22,100
Returns Inwards	€160
Returns Outward	€300
Sales	€34,200
Carriage Inwards	€350
Closing Stock	€6,000
Import Duty	€150

6.

Opening Stock	€3,100
Purchases	€28,000
Sales	€19,000
Closing Stock	€2,400
Carriage Inwards	€200
Returns Inwards	€600
Returns Outwards	€150
NB Gross Loss	

7.

Opening Stock	€6,000
Purchases	€48,250
Sales	€64,350
Sales Returns	€50
Purchases Returns	€1,150
Carriage Inwards	€500
Closing Stock	€7,250

8.

Opening Stock	€250
Purchases	€4,600
Sales	€11,200
Returns Out	€300
Closing Stock	€650
Duty on Purchases	€120

9.

Opening Stock	€14,000
Closing Stock	€16,000
Purchases	€58,400
Sales	€88,000
Returns Inwards	€2,000
Carriage on Purchases	€2,700

10.

Purchases	€12,120
Sales	€41,020
Sales Returns	€1,220
Carriage on Purchases	€190
Duty on Purchases	€90
Purchases Returns	€500
Closing Stock	€4,300

Practice Questions

Profit and Loss Account

In each of the following questions prepare a Profit and Loss Account for the year ended 31 December 2000.

1.

Gross Profit	€19,000
Wages and Salaries	€11,400
Postage and Stationery	€360
Telephone	€760
Heating and Lighting	€980

2.

Gross Profit	€28,000
Insurance	€460
Heating and Lighting	€420
Office Expenses	€1,640
Advertising	€400
Repairs	€400
Telephone	€440
Interest Received	€400
Rent and Rates	€2,600
Wages and Salaries	€16,000.

3.

Gross Profit	€16,000
Travelling Expenses	€4,200
Commission	€2,350
Office Expenses	€840
Rent Received	€3,600
Interest Received	€200
Bad Debts	€400

4.

Gross Profit	€14,000
Interest on Building Society Deposit Account	€1,400
Carriage Out	€1,460
Bank Charges	€80
Repairs to Vehicles	€600
Depreciation: Premises	€900
Telephone	€630
Postage and Stationery	€240
E.S.B.	€480

5.

Gross Profit	€16,800
Postage	€140
Stationery	€80
Salaries	€9,100
Insurance	€310
Bad Debts Recovered	€440
Interest Received	€100
Rent Received	€2,650
Commission Received	€200

6.

Gross Loss	€1,200
Rent Received	€4,000
Interest Received	€100
Salesperson's Commission	€460
Carriage Outwards	€490
Paintings of Buildings	€4,000
Office Expenses	€2,600

7.

Gross Profit	€18,260
Depreciation of Motor Vans	€2,400
Audit and Accounting Fees	€4,000
Showroom Expenses	€200
Bad Debts Recovered	€260
Bank Interest	€250
Bank Charges	€90
Telephone	€600
Postage and Stationery	€280
Insurance	€640
Wages and Salaries	€10,200
Rates	€1,200
Rent Received	€4,800
General Expenses	€680

8.

Gross Profit	€9,600
Interest on Term Loan	€260
Bad Debts	€900
Wages	€7,200
Rent	€1,600
Office Expenses	€400
Heat and Light	€540

Practice Questions

Balance Sheet

Prepare a Balance Sheet in each for each of the following questions.

1.

Share Capital	€60,000
Premises	€40,000
Motor Vans	€18,000
Fixtures and Fittings	€1,500
Office Equipment	€1,800
Debtors	€4,000
Stock	€2,600
Cash	€50
Bank	€1,500
Creditors	€9,450

2.

Share Capital	€70,000
Premises	€60,000
Fixtures and Fittings	€2,000
Plant and Machinery	€7,000
Debtors	€6,500
Stock	€6,500
Creditors	€9,400
Bank Overdraft	€2,600

3.

Share Capital	€85,000
Buildings and Land	€45,000
Building Society Deposit Account	€6,400
Debtors	€9,200
Stock	€13,300
Cash	€90
Creditors	€7,200
Motor Vehicles	€22,000
Bank Overdraft	€3,790

4.

Share Capital	€20,000
Machinery	€3,000
Motor Van	€7,400
Bills Receivable	€600
Debtors	€4,000
Bank	€6,100
Creditors	€2,000
Stock	€900

5.

Share Capital	€50,000
Land and Buildings	€60,000
Fixtures and Fittings	€2,400
Office Equipment	€1,600
Motor Vehicles	€16,400
Debtors	€9,600
Cash	€700
Stock	€11,400
Bank Deposit Account	€2,000
Creditors	€8,100
Bills Payable	€2,000
Proposed Dividends	€5,000
Bank Loan	€30,000
Net Profit	€9,000

6.

Leasehold Premises	€35,000
Motor Vehicles	€16,000
Cash	€60
Petty Cash	€10
Bank	€2,430
Debtors	€4,200
Bills Receivable	€1,400
Bills Payable	€800
Creditors	€3,400
Bank Loan	€16,000
Share Capital	€30,000
Revenue Reserve	€2,000
Net Profit	€6,900

7.

Premises	€40,000
Furniture and Fittings	€5,000
Debtors	€6,000
Closing Stock	€4,000
Cash	€100
Creditors	€5,100
Bank Overdraft	€6,000
Share Capital	€35,000
Bank Loan	€5,000
Revenue Reserve	€1,000
Net Profit	€3,000

8.

Petty Cash	€30
Bank	€4,100
Stock	€3,600
Creditors	€1,900
Bills Payable	€400
Bank Loan	€15,000
Warehouse	€25,100
Motor Van	€11,000
Share Capital	€20,000
Net Profit	€6,530

Practice Questions

Trading, Profit and Loss Account

Prepare a Trading, Profit and Loss Account for each of the following questions.

1.

Sales	€58,000
Carriage In	€200
Customs Duty	€150
Returns Outward	€350
Purchases	€24,000
Opening Stock	€6,400
Closing Stock	€3,400
Rent and Rates	€1,600
Wages and Salaries	€11,400
Interest Received	€160
Bad Debts	€100
Office Expenses	€1,240
Light and Heat	€1,260
Insurance	€550
Advertising	€200
Commission Received	€440

2.

Rent Received	€200
Rates	€600
Opening Stock	€7,100
Closing Stock	€9,600
Sales	€29,000
Purchases	€17,000
Telephone	€505
Postage and Stationery	€340
Returns Out	€2,400
Wages	€6,500
Carriage Out	€200
Bank Charges	€96
Bad Debts Recovered	€220

3.

Interest on Loan	€900
Rent Received	€600
Opening Stock	€4,750
Closing Stock	€6,200
Audit Fees	€600

Sales	€48,740
Purchases	€26,280
Returns In	€900
Returns Out	€280
Carriage In	€200
Import Duty	€300
Postage	€140
Stationery	€80
Depreciation:	
Furniture and Fittings	€150
Motor Vehicles	€1,100
Telephone	€380
Light and Heat	€290

4.

Opening Stock	€1,600
Closing Stock	€4,800
Sales	€24,300
Purchases	€11,400
Office Expenses	€900
Carriage Out	€600
Advertising	€150
Fuel and Light	€180
Insurance	€380
Returns In	€400
Returns Out	€300
Duty on Purchases	€500
Interest on Building	
Society Deposit Account	€1,600
Bad Debt Recovered	€90
Salesperson's Commission	€1,600
Salaries	€14,000

5.

Opening Stock	€3,800
Sales	€78,000
Purchases	€45,000
Closing Stock	€6,600
Carriage In	€900

Import Duty	€1,000
Wages	€10,600
Returns In	€900
Returns Out	€600
Audit Fees	€500
Insurance	€650
Rent and Rates	€3,600
General Expenses	€1,800
Travelling Expenses	€2,400
Interest Received	€960
Bank Charges	€72
Bad Debts	€308

6.

Opening Stock	€950
Purchases	€32,210
Sales	€59,460
Import Duty	€190
Carriage In	€270
Rent Received	€7,800
Rates	€2,400
Packing Materials	€4,700
Office Salaries	€14,300
Audit Fees	€360
Bank Interest	€400
Closing Stock	€4,300
Director's Fees	€8,000
Returns In	€600
Returns Out	€900

7.

Opening Stock	€9,300
Sales	€63,000
Purchases	€28,460
Returns Out	€900
Returns In	€200
Carriage on Sales	€2,400
Import Duty	€500
Depreciation: Machinery	€500
Audit Fees	€380
Bank Charges	€60
Interest on Loan	€1,800
Rent Received	€500

8.

Stock (01 Jan. 1988)	€1,800
Stock (31 Dec. 1983)	€1,600
Purchases	€1,900
Sales	€39,000
Returns In	€500
Customs Duty	€100
Carriage Out	€400
Wages	€400
Office Salaries	€6,400
Office Expenses	€4,600
Bad Debts	€60
Interest Received	€120

9.

Purchases	€28,000
Sales	€35,000
Closing Stock	€2,400
Returns In	€1,500
Carriage on Purchases	€100
Carriage on Sales,	€500
Rent Received	€2,400
Rates	€1,000
Wages and Salaries	€11,500
Bad Debts	€90
Advertising	€600
Showroom Expenses	€900
Repairs	€500
Bank Charges	€90
Bad Debts Recovered	€200

10.

Opening Stock	€2,900
Sales	€18,000
Purchases	€10,000
Closing Stock	€3,400
Wages	€3,300
Office Expenses	€300
Rent Received	€900
Interest Received	€600
Bank Charges	€75
Depreciation: Equipment	€200

Practice Questions

Short Questions — Trading, Profit and Loss Account, Balance Sheet

In each of the following questions prepare a Trading and Profit and Loss Account for the year ended 31 December 1989 and a Balance Sheet as on that date.

1.

	DR €	CR €
Stock 01 Jan. 1989	7,000	
Premises	40,000	
Motor Vehicles	15,000	
Purchases and Sales	28,000	60,000
Debtors and Creditors	9,700	8,000
Returns In and Out	2,100	1,600
Import Duty	200	
Share Capital		35,000
Bank Overdraft		2,520
Office Expenses	2,400	
Insurance	920	
Delivery Expenses	1,600	
Cash	200	
	107,120	107,120

Adjustments:
  (i) Stock 31 December 1989 €6,300
 (ii) Depreciation: Premises 2%, Delivery Vans 12.5%
(iii) Insurance Prepaid €90
 (iv) Office Expenses Due €40

2.

	DR €	CR €
Share Capital		25,000
Buildings	30,000	
Motor Vehicles	18,000	
Equipment	3,000	
Bank Loan		15,000
Purchases and Sales	32,500	61,000
Returns In and Out	2,000	600
Stock 01 Jan. 1989	7,100	
General Expenses	4,900	
Advertising	2,000	
Debtors and Creditors	6,300	4,200
	105,800	105,800

Adjustments:
  (i) Closing Stock €6,000
  (ii) Depreciation: Motor Vehicles 15%
  (iii) Advertising Prepaid €500
  (iv) General Expenses Due €100

3.

	DR €	CR €
Share Capital		49,000
Premises	45,000	
Motor Vehicles	16,000	
Stock 01 Jan. 1989	7,200	
Purchases and Sales	17,000	39,000
Wages	6,000	
Debtors and Creditors	5,900	6,100
Returns In and Out	800	200
Rent Received		2,600
General Expenses	1,400	
Office Expenses	2,600	
Bank Loan		5,000
	101,900	99,300

Adjustments:
  (i) Stock 31 Dec. 1989 €5,000
  (ii) Office Expenses Prepaid €40
  (iii) General Expenses Due €15
  (iv) Depreciation: Motor Vehicles 10%

4.

	DR €	CR €
Share Capital		62,000
Land and Buildings	60,000	
Equipment and Machinery	15,000	
Purchases and Sales	37,000	64,000
Delivery Expenses	3,800	
Import Duty	200	
Carriage Inwards	100	
Bank Overdraft		2,100
Rent Received		5,000
Debtors and Creditors	12,000	7,000
Stock 01 Jan. 1989	11,000	
Postage and Stationery	380	
Light and Heat	620	
	140,100	140,100

Adjustments:
  (i) Stock 31 Dec. 1989 €9,200
 (ii) Depreciation: Equipment and Machinery 8%
(iii) Light and Heat Due €50

5.

	DR €	CR €
Share Capital		48,000
Debtors and Creditors	16,000	9,000
Carriage In	300	
Stock 01 Jan. 1989	7,400	
Postage and Stationery	220	
Purchases and Sales	28,000	42,000
Premises	25,000	
Motor Vehicles	11,000	
Bills Payable	800	
Bank Overdraft		920
Bank Interest and Charges	460	
Cash	200	
Bad Debts Recovered		400
Equipment	10,940	
	100,320	100,320

Adjustments:
  (i) Closing Stock €9,600
 (ii) Depreciation: Motor Vehicles 10%, Equipment 8%
(iii) Stock of Postage Stamps on Hand €10

6.

	DR €	CR €
Buildings	34,000	
Equipment	6,000	
Motor Expenses	4,200	
Rent of Motor Van	3,900	
Purchases and Sales	78,000	124,000
Stock 01 Jan. 1989	19,000	
Advertising	700	
Debtors and Creditors	7,000	10,800
Office Expenses	1,900	
Share Capital		20,000
Cash	100	
	154,800	154,800

Adjustments:
  (i) Closing Stock €15,600
  (ii) Offices Expenses Due €200
  (iii) Depreciation: Equipment 5%

7.

	DR €	CR €
Share Capital		16,700
Debtors and Creditors	7,200	6,190
Purchases and Sales	48,400	65,300
Light and Heat	1,280	
Delivery Expenses	6,300	
Postage and Stationery	180	
Telephone	630	
Rent	900	
Motor Vehicles	12,000	
Equipment	4,000	
Stock 01 Jan. 1989	7,300	
	88,190	88,190

Adjustments:
  (i) Closing Stock €9,200
  (ii) Depreciation: Motor Vehicles 12.5%
  (iii) Rent Due €120
  (iv) Stock of Stationery on Hand €30

8.

	DR €	CR €
Debtors and Creditors	7,300	2,100
Purchases and Sales	96,240	128,300
Wages	15,200	
Buildings	44,000	
Telephone	2,160	
Interest Received		630
Stock 01 Jan. 1989	17,000	
Furniture and Fittings	7,000	
Packing and Freight Charges	3,600	
Share Capital		55,000
Import Duty	530	
Bank		800
	186,830	186,830

Adjustments:
  (i) Closing Stock €14,400
 (ii) Provide for Dividends of 6%
(iii) Depreciation: Furniture and Fittings 5%

9.

	DR €	CR €
Furniture	2,600	
Telephone	1,400	
Debtors and Creditors	6,300	5,900
Purchases and Sales	28,240	47,360
Bad Debts	220	
Buildings	60,000	
Rent		700
Rates	2,460	
Stock 01 Jan. 1989	4,920	
Insurance	480	
Motor Vehicles	16,000	
Share Capital		65,000
Bank		3,660
	122,620	122,620

Adjustments:
  (i) Stock 31 January 1989 €5,700
 (ii) Depreciation: Motor Vehicles 15%
(iii) Insurance Prepaid €60

10.

	DR €	CR €
Furniture	6,200	
Buildings	80,000	
Debtors and Creditors	6,200	7,100
Purchases and Sales	69,000	101,200
Stock 01 Jan. 1989	11,200	
Rent of Motor Vehicles	2,300	
Motor Vehicle Expenses	1,900	
General Expenses	4,620	
Carriage In	1,600	
Share Capital		70,000
Bank		5,140
Bank Interest	420	
	183,440	183,440

Adjustments:
  (i) Closing Stock €13,100
 (ii) Depreciation: Furniture 5%
(iii) Provide for Dividends 10%
(iv) General Expenses Paid in Advance €120

11.

	DR €	CR €
Insurance	240	
Buildings	75,000	
Motor Vehicles	25,000	
Purchases and Sales	220,000	334,000
Stock 01 Jan. 1989	44,000	
Wages	28,000	
Carriage In	2,240	
Debtors and Creditors	31,020	19,600
General Expenses	16,280	
Office Expenses	11,600	
Bank Loan		20,000
Bank Overdraft		4,260
Bank Interest and Charges	3,560	
Audit Fees	920	
Share Capital		80,000
	457,860	457,860

Adjustments:
  (i) Closing Stock €49,800
 (ii) Office Expenses Due €1,400
(iii) General Expenses Prepaid €940
(iv) Depreciation: Motor Vehicles 10%

12.

	DR €	CR €
Buildings	40,000	
Wages and Salaries	11,800	
Showroom Expenses	1,600	
Advertising	460	
Purchases and Sales	24,000	47,220
Debtors and Creditors	7,200	5,900
Stock 01 Jan. 1989	8,100	
Machinery	12,500	
Telephone	580	
Share Capital		50,000
Bank		3,120
	106,240	106,240

Adjustments:
  (i) Closing Stock €8,350
 (ii) Advertising Prepaid €95
(iii) Depreciation: Machinery 10%

13.

	DR €	CR €
Insurance	570	
Debtors and Creditors	6,300	7,150
Purchases and Sales	54,200	63,220
Buildings	90,000	
Motor Vehicles	25,000	
Bad Debts	490	
Rent Received		2,400
Share Capital		100,000
Stock 01 Jan.1989	7,600	
Audit Fees	620	
VAT	510	
Light and Heat	2,450	
Office Expenses	1,340	
Revenue Reserve		16,310
	189,080	189,080

Adjustments:
   (i) Closing Stock €8,300
  (ii) Depreciation: Motor Vehicles 15%
 (iii) Rent Receivable Outstanding €120
 (iv) Light and Heat Prepaid €160
  (v) Office Expenses Due €90
 (vi) Provide for Dividends 5%

14.

	DR €	CR €
Buildings	78,000	
Purchases and Sales	29,200	45,600
General Expenses	4,100	
Repairs	1,900	
Debtors and Creditors	6,800	5,700
Interest Received		860
VAT		1,600
Share Capital		85,000
Revenue Reserve		6,020
Bank	19,180	
Stock 01 Jan. 1989	5,600	
	144,780	144,780

Adjustments:

(i) Closing Stock €6,210

(ii) Transfer Profit to Revenue Reserve

(iii) General Expenses Due €300

15.

	DR €	CR €
Stock 01 Jan. 1989	7,000	
Premises	60,000	
Motor Vehicles	16,000	
Purchases and Sales	47,200	76,320
Debtors and Creditors	5,900	6,300
Rates	3,120	
Carriage In	380	
Office Expenses	4,210	
Cash	590	
Revenue Reserve		11,780
Share Capital		50,000
	144,400	144,400

Adjustments:

(i) Closing Stock €9,200

(ii) Depreciation: Premises 2%, Motor Vehicles 10%

(iii) Rates Prepaid €320

(iv) Office Expenses Due €145

(v) Provide Dividends of 13%

(vi) Transfer Balance of Profit to Revenue Reserve

16.

	DR €	CR €
Premises	55,000	
Showroom Expenses	2,100	
Debtors and Creditors	5,940	6,210
Purchases and Sales	49,320	64,600
Stock 01 Jan. 1989	7,180	
General Expenses	7,460	
Bank	4,100	
Bank Interest Received		408
Revenue Reserve		4,882
Share Capital		55,000
	131,100	131,100

Adjustments:
  (i) Closing Stock €8,320
 (ii) Provide for Dividends of 12%
(iii) General Expenses Due €280
(iv) Transfer of Profit or Loss to Revenue Reserve

Practice Questions

Long Questions — Trading, Profit and Loss Account, Balance Sheets

1. Prepare the Trading and Profit and Loss Account of S. Barron and Co. Ltd. for the year ended 30 June 1988 and a Balance Sheet on that date. Authorised and Issued Share Capital 42,100 €1 Ordinary Shares.

	DR €	CR €
Premises	50,000	
Delivery Vans	18,000	
Debtors and Creditors	5,000	9,010
Purchases and Sales	28,000	55,000
Rent Received		1,000
Insurance	600	
Carriage In	200	
Import Duty	300	
Stocks 01 July 1987	4,200	
Returns In and Out	400	500
Bank Charges	160	
Bank	2,200	
Petty Cash	50	
Building Society Loan		8,000
General Expenses	400	
Postage and Stationery	500	
Furniture and Fittings	4,000	
Interest on Building Society Loan	600	
Light and Heat	900	
Issued Share Capital €1 Shares		42,000
	115,510	115,510

Adjustments:
   (i) Closing Stock €5,100
  (ii) Insurance Prepaid €100
 (iii) General Expenses Due €50
  (iv) Depreciation: Premises 2%, Delivery Vans 10%

2. Prepare the Trading Account and Profit and Loss Account of J. O'Donovan, Ltd, for the year ended 31 March 1989 and a Balance Sheet as on that date. Authorised and Issued Share Capital 35,000 €1 Ordinary Shares.

	DR €	CR €
Purchases and Sales	19,000	45,000
Wages	7,000	
Premises	35,000	
Motor Vehicles	16,000	
Plant and Machinery	21,000	
Bills Payable		6,000
Debtors and Creditors	4,400	9,600
Returns In and Out	900	2,200
Office Expenses	1,400	
Insurance	540	
Advertising	380	
Bad Debts	220	
Stock 01 Apr. 1988	5,000	
Rates	1,000	
Bank Charges	126	
Import Duty	600	
Petty Cash	34	
Loan		15,500
Interest on Loan	400	
Commission	300	
Share Capital		35,000
	113,300	113,300

Adjustments:
  (i) Closing Stock €6,000
 (ii) A Dividend of 4% to be Paid
(iii) Advertising Prepaid €45
(iv) Loan Interest Due €800
 (v) Depreciation: Motor Vehicles 20%, Plant and Machinery 12%

3. Prepare the Trading and Profit and Loss Account of J. Connors Ltd., for the year ended 30 September 1989 and a Balance Sheet as on that date. Authorised and Issued Share Capital 60,000 €1 Ordinary shares.

	DR €	CR €
Rent and Rates	4,600	
Purchases and Sales	28,000	53,200
Premises	40,000	
Motor Vehicles	19,000	
Audit Fees	2,000	
Telephone	1,350	
Import Duty	400	
Carriage on Sales	1,600	
Advertising	3,600	
Insurance	300	
Motor Vehicle Insurance	900	
Bills Payable		3,600
Debtors and Creditors	5,400	3,900
Stock 01 Oct. 1988	3,200	
Returns In and Out	900	600
Wages	7,000	
Office Equipment	4,000	
Furniture and Fittings	5,000	
Cash	100	
Bank	4,800	
Stationery	500	
Interest Received		290
Revenue Reserve		11,060
Ordinary Share Capital		60,000
	132,650	132,650

Adjustments:
  (i) Closing Stock €7,900
 (ii) Interest Receivable Outstanding €190
(iii) Stock of Stationery 30 Sept. 1989 €120
 (iv) Telephone Due €70
  (v) Insurance Prepaid €50
 (vi) Depreciation: Motor Vehicles 15%, Office Equipment 10%

4. Prepare the Trading and Profit and Loss Account of S. Cliffe Ltd, for the year ended 31 October 1989 and a Balance Sheet as on that date. Authorised Share Capital 100,000 €1 Ordinary Shares.

	DR €	CR €
Plant and Machinery	40,000	
Motor Vehicles	24,000	
Rent of Premises	9,000	
Wages and Salaries	14,000	
Stock 01 Nov. 1988	3,900	
Office Expenses	2,400	
Directors' Fees	8,000	
Bank Charges	180	
Delivery Expenses	2,460	
Carriage In	1,410	
Purchases and Sales	34,360	89,280
Returns In and Out	2,220	1,400
Bad Debts Recovered		290
Debtors and Creditors	9,400	15,200
Bank		1,600
Bank Loan		5,000
Repairs of Motor Vehicle	540	
Insurance	4,400	
Advertising	1,500	
Ordinary Share Capital		45,000
	157,770	157,770

Adjustments:
  (i) Stock 31 Oct. 1989 €16,800
 (ii) Provide for Interest on Bank Loan 8%
(iii) Insurance Prepaid €200
 (iv) Provide for a Dividend of 6%
  (v) Depreciation: Plant and Machinery 10%, Motor Vehicles 14%

5. Prepare a Trading and Profit and Loss Account of P. Dunne Ltd for the year ended 30 November 1988 and a Balance Sheet as on that date. Authorised Share Capital 100,000 €1 Ordinary Shares.

	DR €	CR €
Premises	90,000	
Rent		7,200
Motor Vehicles	16,000	
Rates	2,400	
Stock 01 Dec. 1988	14,380	
Purchases and Sales	48,200	79,600
V.A.T.	300	
Sales Returns	400	
Carriage In	300	
Light and Heat	2,400	
Telephone	900	
General Expenses	1,600	
Debtors and Creditors	5,200	7,900
Petty Cash	50	
Bank Deposit Account	4,000	
Interest Received		400
Bills Receivable	3,400	
Insurance	900	
Showroom Expenses	1,500	
Audit Fees	1,050	
Director's Fees	1,200	
Bills Payable		4,000
Revenue Reserve		15,080
Issued Share Capital		80,000
	194,180	194,180

Adjustments:
  (i) Closing Stock €9,600
 (ii) Rates Prepaid €800
(iii) Stock of Heating Oil on Hand €300
 (iv) Telephone Due €360
  (v) Provide for a Dividend of 3%
 (vi) Depreciation: Motor Vehicles 15%

6. Prepare a Trading, and Profit and Loss Account of J. Flynn Ltd, for the year ended 31 December 1989 and a Balance Sheet as on that date. Authorised and Issued Share Capital 75,000 €1 Ordinary Shares.

	DR €	CR €
Issued Share Capital		75,000
Premises	50,000	
Rent of Van	3,000	
Plant and Machinery	5,800	
Office Equipment	1,400	
Purchases and Sales	34,000	89,000
Stock 01 Jan. 1989	7,400	
Carriage on Sales	200	
Stationery	320	
Light and Heat	735	
Returns		400
Bad Debts Recovered		380
Insurance	300	
Telephone	920	
Debtors and Creditors	4,200	6,300
Import Duty	360	
Wages and Salaries	9,080	
Director's Fees	11,500	
Bank Current Account	2,065	
Bank Deposit Account	39,800	
	171,080	171,080

Adjustments:
  (i) Closing Stock €9,890
 (ii) Stock of Stationery 31 Dec. 1989 €70
(iii) Interest Due on Deposit Account €1,800
 (iv) Provide for Dividends of 6%
  (v) Provide for Depreciation Plant and Machinery 10%

7. Prepare a Trading and Profit and Loss Account of R. McGrath Ltd. for the year ended 31 December 1987 and a Balance Sheet as on that date. Authorised Share Capital 60,000 €1 Ordinary Shares.

	DR €	CR €
Stock 01 Jan. 1987	10,000	
Issued Share Capital		55,000
Premises	60,000	
Fixtures and Fittings	5,000	
Telephone	2,000	
Vehicles	15,800	
Rates	1,400	
Purchases and Sales	48,000	79,300
Office Equipment	2,000	
Office Expenses	3,600	
Carriage In	500	
Returns	600	
Bills Payable		4,400
Rent		5,500
Bad Debts Recovered		260
Advertising	2,420	
Painting of Premises	5,000	
Rent of Machinery	1,500	
Bank Charges	900	
Legal Expenses	650	
Debtors and Creditors	20,900	5,000
Bank Loan		30,000
Bank Overdraft		810
	180,270	180,270

Adjustments:
  (i) Interest Due on Bank Overdraft €40
 (ii) Provide for Interest on Bank Loan at 12.5% per annum
(iii) Provide for Depreciation on Vehicles 15%
 (iv) Provide for Dividends 8%
  (v) Rates Prepaid €200
 (vi) Closing Stock €6,000

8. Prepare a Trading and Profit and Loss Account of R. Lynch Ltd for the year ended 01 March 1989 and a Balance Sheet as on that date. Authorised Share Capital 100,000 €1 Ordinary Shares.

	DR €	CR €
Share Capital		80,000
Premises	140,000	
Term Loan from Bank		70,000
Rent of Vehicles	12,000	
Advertising	8,900	
Petrol and Oil	6,800	
Insurance of Vehicles	2,650	
Debtors and Creditors	18,070	9,500
Bad Debts	1,680	
Office Equipment	1,900	
Purchases and Sales	74,000	128,600
Returns In and Out	200	1,500
Stock 01 Apr. 1988	14,800	
Machinery	8,600	
Cash	220	
Bank	1,050	
Packing Materials	8,300	
Rent		2,300
Audit Fees	260	
V.A.T.		3,400
Interest on Loan	4,200	
Revenue Reserve		8,330
	303,630	303,630

Adjustments:
 (i) Closing Stock €16,200
 (ii) Depreciation: Office Equipment 6%
 (iii) Provide for Dividend of 7%
 (iv) Transfer Balance of Profit to Revenue Reserve
 (v) Stock of Packing Materials 31 Mar. 1989 €1,100
 (vi) Insurance Prepaid €350

9. Prepare a Trading and Profit and Loss Account of D. Walsh Ltd for the year ended 30 April 1989 and a Balance Sheet as on that date. Authorised Share Capital 66,000 €1 Ordinary Shares.

	DR €	CR €
Stock 01 May 1989	4,300	
Purchases and Sales	47,000	63,000
Debtors and Creditors	9,400	6,100
Bank Overdraft		6,200
Import Duty	300	
Carriage on Purchases	420	
Advertising	800	
Wages and Salaries	14,600	
Director's Fees	2,000	
Patents	15,000	
Premises	38,000	
Fixtures and Fittings	6,000	
Equipment	7,500	
Motor Van	9,000	
Bad Debts	60	
Bank Charges	90	
Salesperson's Commission	1,700	
Revenue Reserve		11,400
Returns	200	4,600
Bills Receivable	600	
Postage and Telephone	330	
Issued Shared Capital		66,000
	157,300	157,300

Adjustments:
  (i) Stock 30 Apr. 1989 €5,700
 (ii) Interest Due Bank Overdraft €730
(iii) Depreciation: Motor Van 10%
 (iv) Import Duty Due €100
  (v) Transfer Net Profit or Loss to Revenue Reserve

10. Prepare a Trading and Profit and Loss Account of P. Walton Ltd for the year ended 31 December 1988 and a Balance Sheet as on that date. Authorised Share Capital 50,000 €1 Ordinary Shares.

	DR €	CR €
Leasehold Premises	58,000	
Goodwill	5,000	
Telephone	960	
Advertising	6,220	
Patents	8,000	
Bills Payable		3,600
Stock 01 Jan. 1988	1,980	
Delivery Vans	18,000	
Delivery Vans Expenses	4,980	
Machinery	14,000	
Bank Loan		60,000
Cash	100	
Bank Overdraft		2,200
Interest on Bank Overdraft	190	
Bank Charges	80	
Legal Fees	440	
Debtors and Creditors	3,800	4,900
Purchases and Sales	27,000	47,620
Returns	420	
Carriage In	900	
Insurance	460	
Postage and Stationery	370	
Director's Fees	500	
Revenue Reserve		3,080
Share Capital		30,000
	151,400	151,400

Adjustments:
(i) Stock 31 Dec. 1988 €9,760
(ii) Provide for Dividends of 2.5%
(iii) Depreciation: Delivery Vans 12%, Machinery 6%
(iv) Provide for Interest on Bank Loan 10%
(v) Stock of Postage Stamps 31 Dec. 1988 €20

11. Prepare a Trading and Profit and Loss Account of P. Breathnach Ltd for the year ended 30 November 1989 and a Balance Sheet as on that date. Authorised Share Capital 200,000 €1 Ordinary Shares.

	DR €	CR €
Premises	80,000	
Telephone	500	
Bank Deposit Account	6,000	
Debtors and Creditors	4,200	9,300
Cash	180	
Stock 01 Dec. 1988	7,980	
Purchases and Sales	17,000	69,000
Wages and Salaries	18,000	
Salaries	14,000	
Director's Fees	6,000	
Dividends	4,000	
Motor Vehicles	29,000	
Interest on Deposit Account		300
Rent		4,160
Rates	3,100	
Fixtures and Fittings	7,000	
Machinery	18,000	
Office Expenses	4,950	
Light and Heat	8,900	
Revenue Reserve		66,050
Issued Share Capital		80,000
	228,810	228,810

Adjustments:
  (i) Stock 30 November 1988 €6,725
 (ii) Depreciation: Premises 2%, Motor Vehicles 10%
(iii) Transfer Balance of Profit and Loss Account to Revenue Reserve
 (iv) Interest Receivable Due on Deposit Account €100
  (v) Office Expenses Prepaid €250

12. Prepare a Trading and Profit and Loss Account of K. Kiely Ltd for the year ended 31 December 1988 and a Balance Sheet as on that date. Authorised Share Capital 150,000 €1 Ordinary Shares.

	DR €	CR €
Buildings	80,000	
Fixtures and Fittings	16,000	
Customs Duty	400	
Telephone	3,600	
Purchases and Sales	120,000	194,600
Debtors and Creditors	24,000	18,000
Stock 01 Jan. 1988	29,280	
Post and Stationery	1,460	
Packing Materials	2,790	
Advertising	12,000	
Bank		7,920
Bank Charges	520	
Bank Interest	710	
Bad Debts Recovered		4,000
Bad Debts	1,100	
Rent and Rates	14,000	
Light and Heat	9,400	
Rent of Motor Vehicles	9,600	
Insurance	400	
Wages and Salaries	34,000	
Revenue Reserve		34,740
Issued Share Capital		100,000
	359,260	359,260

Adjustments:
  (i) Stock 31 December 1988 €35,760
 (ii) Provide for Dividends 3%
(iii) Postage Stamps on Hand €70
 (iv) Packing Materials 31 December 1988 €880
  (v) Advertising Prepaid €8,000
 (vi) Rent and Rates Due €900

13. Prepare a Trading and Profit and Loss Account of M. Fitzgerald Ltd for the year ended 31 January 1990 and a Balance Sheet as on that date. Authorised Share Capital 10,000 €1 Ordinary Shares.

	DR €	CR €
Rent of Building	2,000	
Rates	460	
Light and Heat	480	
Postage and Stationery	190	
Bank	5,000	
Motor Vehicle	7,000	
Equipment	700	
Debtors and Creditors	460	390
Purchases and Sales	9,220	22,200
Stock 01 Feb. 1989	5,100	
Insurance	790	
Bank Interest		400
Bad Debts Recovered		120
Showroom Expenses	360	
Advertising	200	
Petty Cash	50	
Bills Receivable	900	
Revenue Reserve		800
Issued Share Capital		9,000
	32,910	32,910

Adjustments:
  (i) Stock 31 Jan. 1990 €6,300
 (ii) Depreciation: Motor Vehicles 10%, Equipment 5%
(iii) Provide for Dividends 13%
 (iv) Rates Prepaid €120
  (v) Light Bill Due €60
 (vi) Bank Interest Receivable Outstanding €50
(vii) Provide for Director's Fees €500
(viii) Transfer Balance of Net Profit to General Reserve

Trading, Profit and Loss Account, Balance Sheet

1. The following Trial Balance was extracted from the books of Hartnett Ltd on 31 May 1989.

(A) You are required to prepare the company's Trading, Profit and Loss and Appropriation Accounts for the year ended 31 May 1989 and a Balance Sheet as that date. The Authorised Share Capital is €100,000 Ordinary Shares.

TRIAL BALANCE

	DR €	CR €
Purchases and Sales	74,000	142,000
VAT	600	
Debtors and Creditors	6,900	7,200
Sales Returns and Purchases Returns	2,100	4,800
Bad Debts	400	
Rent Receivable		6,800
Carriage Inwards	3,600	
Wages and Salaries	19,300	
10 Year Loan		10,000
Plant and Machinery at Cost	24,000	
Bank Overdraft		3,600
Opening Stock 01 June 1988	16,000	
Buildings at Cost	80,000	
Insurance	4,600	
Cash	700	
Bank Interest	500	
Import Duty	2,900	
Issued Share Capital		60,000
	235,000	235,000

Additional Information 31 May 1989:
(i) Closing Stock €17,000
(ii) Rent Receivable Prepaid €1,200
(iii) Insurance Due €1,200
(iv) Dividends Declared 8%
(v) Depreciation: Buildings 2%, Plant and Machinery 10%

(B) How might a company reduce bad debts?

2. The following Trial Balance was extracted from the books of Waters Ltd on 31 March 1997. The Authorised Share Capital is 200,000 €1 Ordinary Shares.

(A) You are required to prepare the company's Trading, Profit and Loss and Appropriation Accounts for the year ended 31 March 1997 and a Balance Sheet as at that date.

TRIAL BALANCE

	DR €	CR €
Purchases and Sales	79,000	157,000
Advertising	7,000	
Bank Interest	2,400	
Furniture and Fittings	14,000	
Dividends Paid	17,000	
Buildings	130,000	
Sales Returns	3,400	
Carriage Inwards	2,800	
Light and Heat	4,600	
Wages	26,000	
Debtors and Creditors	13,200	11,400
Bank Term Loan		13,200
Opening Stock 01 Apr. 1996	14,600	
Commission Receivable		8,400
Motor Vehicles	26,000	
Issued Share Capital		150,000
	€340,000	€340,000

Additional Information on 31 March 1997:
   (i) Closing Stock €15,300
  (ii) Carriage Inwards Due €700
 (iii) Advertising Prepaid €2,000
 (iv) Depreciation: Furniture and Fittings 5%, Motor Vehicles 16%

(B) Calculate the return on Capital Employed. Show your calculations.

3. The following balances were extracted from the books of Sheridan Ltd on the 30 June 1995. The Authorised Share Capital is 200,000 €1 Ordinary Shares.

(A) You are required to prepare the company's Profit and Loss and Appropriation Accounts for the year ended 30 June 1995 and a Balance Sheet as at that date.

	€
Gross Profit	86,250
Wages	18,000
Advertising	5,000
Insurance	3,500
Interest Receivable	750
Bank Deposit Account	15,000
Light and Heat	3,800
Premises	118,000
Machinery	30,000
Debtors	12,000
Creditors	8,000
Cash	250
Motor Vans	30,000
Bank Overdraft	1,000
Issued Share Capital €1 Shares	130,000
Reserves Profit and Loss Balance (1 July 1994)	11,350

You are given the following information as at 30 June 1995:
  (i) Closing Stock €1,800
 (ii) Interest Receivable Due €150
(iii) Insurance Prepaid €300
(iv) Dividend Declared 4%
 (v) Wages Due €2,000
(vi) Depreciation: Machinery 10%, Motor Vans 20%

(B) Calculate the return on Capital Employed. Show your workings.

4. The following Trial Balance was extracted from the books of Lane Ltd on 30 June 1994. The Authorised Share Capital is 280,000 €1 Ordinary Shares.

(A) You are required to prepare the company's Trading, Profit and Loss and Appropriation Accounts for the year ended 30 June 1994, and a Balance Sheet as at that date.

TRIAL BALANCE

	DR €	CR €
Ordinary Share Capital 260,000 €1 shares		260,000
Premises	120,000	
Motor Vehicles	85,000	
Debtors and Creditors	34,400	19,200
Purchases and Sales	79,000	189,000
Sales Returns and Purchases Returns	3,200	5,500
Wages	26,200	
Import Duty	6,250	
Office Equipment	6,000	
Machinery	74,000	
Rates	11,600	
Insurance	5,800	
Commission Receivable		6,400
Bank	17,550	
Opening Stock 01 July 1993	14,000	
Reserves (Profit and Loss Balance 01 July 1993)		2,900
	483,000	483,000

You are given the following information as at 30 June 1994:
  (i) Closing Stock €17,250
 (ii) Import Duty Due €250
(iii) Rates Prepaid €600
 (iv) Dividends Declared 9%
  (v) Depreciation: Machinery 15%, Office Equipment 12%, Motor Vehicles 20%

(B) Give two possible reasons for Sales Returns.

5. The following Trial Balance was extracted from the books of Ryan Ltd on 30 June 1996. The Authorised Share Capital is 120,000 €1 Ordinary Shares.

(A) You are required to prepare the company's Trading, Profit and Loss and Appropriation Accounts for the year ended 30 June 1996 and a Balance Sheet as at that date.

TRIAL BALANCE

	DR €	CR €
Purchases and Sales	69,000	161,000
Dividends Paid	18,000	
Sales Returns and Purchases Returns	3,400	1,600
Debtors and Creditors	13,200	7,450
Issued Share Capital 90,000 €1 Shares		90,000
Long Term Loan		70,000
Bank Overdraft		3,950
Premises	80,000	
Rent Receivable		8,000
Wages	22,050	
Machinery	50,000	
Motor Vans	70,000	
Carriage Inwards	4,600	
Insurance	3,350	
Opening Stock 01 July 1995	7,400	
Cash	400	
Bank Interest	600	
	342,000	342,000

You are given the following information as at 30 June 1996:
   (i) Closing Stock €8,200
  (ii) Carriage Inwards Due €200
 (iii) Insurance Prepaid €150
 (iv) Depreciation: Machinery 12%, Motor Vans 15%

(B) Calculate the rate of dividend paid to the shareholders of Ryan Ltd.

6. The following Trial Balance was extracted from the books of Shaw Hardware Ltd on 31 July 1995. The Authorised Share Capital is 250,000 €1 Ordinary Shares.

(A) You are required to prepare the Company's Trading, Profit and Loss and Appropriation Accounts for the year ended 31 May 1993 and a Balance Sheet at that date.

TRIAL BALANCE

	DR €	CR €
Issued Share Capital 200,000 €1 Shares		200,000
Bank	10,000	
Buildings	120,000	
Rent Receivable		16,000
Motor Vehicles at Cost	48,000	
Purchases and Sales	82,000	169,500
Opening Stock 01 Aug. 1994	14,000	
Cash	1,000	
Sales Returns	400	
Carriage Inwards	2,500	
Wages	18,500	
Dividends Paid	32,000	
Long Term Loan		14,000
Insurance	2,650	
Light and Heat	2,450	
Equipment at Cost	70,000	
Debtors and Creditors	6,000	10,000
	409,500	409,500

You are given the following additional information on 31 July 1995.
- (i) Closing Stock €19,000
- (ii) Light and Heat Due €650
- (iii) Carriage Inwards Prepaid €600
- (iv) Wages Due €500
- (v) Depreciation: Equipment 20%, Motor Vehicles 15%

(B) Name two types of security a bank would accept when giving a person a loan.

7. The following Trial Balance was extracted from the books of Dowling Ltd on 31 December 1995.

(A) You are required to prepare the Company's Trading, Profit and Loss and Appropriation Account for the year ended 31 December 1995 and a Balance Sheet as at that date. The Authorised Share Capital is 350,000 €1 Ordinary Shares.

TRIAL BALANCE

	DR €	CR €
Issued Share Capital 140,000 €1 Ordinary Shares		140,000
15 Year Loan		50,000
Motor Vans	65,000	
Buildings	120,000	
Purchases and Sales	55,000	100,000
Advertising	2,000	
Bad Debts	1,000	
Carriage Outwards	750	
Debtors and Creditors	44,000	16,650
Sales Returns and Purchases Returns	400	900
Bank Overdraft		8,650
Opening Stock 01 Jan. 1995	27,000	
Commission Received		4,800
Import Duty on Purchases	1,450	
Cash	800	
Light and Heat	3,600	
	321,000	321,000

You are given the following additional information as on 31 December 1995:
  (i) Closing Stock €46,400
  (ii) Advertising Due €600
  (iii) Dividends Declared 15%
  (iv) Commission Received Due €400
  (v) Depreciation: Motor Vans 15%, Buildings 2%

(B) Calculate (i) the Working Capital Ratio (ii) Acid Test Ratio

8. The following Trial Balance was extracted from the books of Irwin Ltd on 31 May 1996.

(A) You are required to prepare the company's Trading, Profit and Loss and Appropriation Accounts for the year ended 31 May 1996, and a Balance Sheet as at that date. The Authorised Share Capital is 250,000 €1 Ordinary Shares.

TRIAL BALANCE

	DR €	CR €
Opening Stock 01 June 1995	16,800	
Issued Share Capital 180,000 €1 Shares		180,000
Purchases and Sales	90,000	185,600
Bad Debts	4,200	
Carriage Inwards	2,800	
Debtors and Creditors	48,000	36,000
Bank Interest	400	
Bank Overdraft		3,600
Wages and Salaries	42,000	
Sales Returns and Purchases Returns	3,200	4,800
Rent Receivable		6,800
Insurance	7,200	
Machinery at Cost	100,000	
Cash	600	
Long Term Loan		50,000
Buildings at Cost	150,000	
Accountant's Fees	1,600	
	466,800	466,800

You are given the following additional information on 31 May 1996:
  (i) Closing Stock 17,800
  (ii) Bank Interest Due 4,000
  (iii) Dividends Declared 8%
  (iv) Rent Receivable Prepaid €300
  (v) Depreciation: Machinery 20%, Buildings 2%

(B) Suggest three ways in which the company might reduce bad debts in the future.

9. The following Trial Balance was extracted from the books of McGrath Ltd on 31 December 1996. The Authorised Share Capital is 300,000 €1 Ordinary Shares.

(A) You are required to prepare the company's Trading, Profit and Loss and Appropriation Accounts for the year ended 31 December 1996 and a Balance Sheet as at that date.

TRIAL BALANCE

	DR €	CR €
Purchases and Sales	89,000	159,600
Issued Share Capital		140,000
Wages	27,500	
Long Term Loan		50,000
Opening Stock 01 Jan. 1996	14,000	
Carriage Inwards	3,500	
Rent Receivable		15,000
Machinery	50,000	
Repairs	4,400	
Cash	600	
Bank Overdraft		2,400
Reserves (Profit and Loss Balance)		4,600
Motor Vans	80,000	
Debtors and Creditors	17,000	21,000
Sales Returns and Purchases Returns	1,000	3,400
Advertising	9,000	
Premises	100,000	
	396,000	396,000

You are given the following information as at 31 December 1996:
  (i) Closing Stock €18,000
 (ii) Dividends Declared 6%
(iii) Advertising Prepaid €3,400
(iv) Rent Receivable Prepaid €1,000
 (v) Depreciation: Machinery 8%, Motor Vans 12%

(B) List three advantages of Stocktaking for McGrath's Company.

10. The following Trial Balance was extracted from the books of Keane Ltd on 31 January 1997. The Authorised Share Capital is 400,000 €1 Ordinary Shares.

(A) You are required to prepare the company's Trading, Profit and Loss and Appropriation Accounts for the year ended 31 January 1997 and a Balance Sheet as at that date.

TRIAL BALANCE

	DR €	CR €
Interest Receivable		4,800
Reserves (Profit and Loss Balance)		45,000
Cash	2,200	
Bank	8,750	
Equipment	70,000	
Insurance	4,300	
Rent	14,600	
Premises	100,000	
Motor Vehicles	80,000	
Purchases and Sales	73,000	162,000
Wages	28,000	
Sales Returns and Purchases Returns	2,500	1,000
Stock 01 Feb. 1996	15,000	
Debtors and Creditors	24,700	13,200
Carriage Inwards	2950	
Ordinary Share Capital		200,000
	426,000	426,000

You are given the following information as at 31 January 1997:
  (i) Closing Stock €16,400
 (ii) Carriage Inwards Due €400
(iii) Insurance Prepaid €450
 (iv) Dividends Declared 8%
  (v) Depreciation: Motor Vehicles 20%, Equipment 12%

(B) Why is it important for companies to have reserves?

11. The following Trial Balance was extracted from the books of O'Driscoll Ltd on 28 February 1997. The Authorised Share Capital is 150,000 €1 Ordinary Shares.

(A) You are required to prepare the company's Trading, Profit and Loss and Appropriation Accounts for the year ended 28 February 1997 and a Balance Sheet as at that date.

TRIAL BALANCE

	DR €	CR €
Purchases and Sales	72,000	135,000
Debtors and Creditors	6,300	7,100
Long Term Loan		50,000
Cash	150	
Bank Interest	900	
Rent Receivable		5,000
Import Duty	1,200	
Sales Returns and Purchases Returns	2,700	1,500
Machinery	30,000	
Bank Overdraft		15,050
Dividends Paid	6,000	
Wages	18,000	
Premises	120,000	
Insurance	4,400	
Opening Stock 01 Mar. 1996	12,000	
Motor Vans	40,000	
Issued Share Capital		100,000
	313,650	313,650

You are given the following information on 28 February 1997:
  (i) Closing Stock €14,400
 (ii) Import Duty Due €300
(iii) Wages Prepaid €500
(iv) Depreciation: Motor Vans 15%, Machinery 12%

(B) Calculate the Working Capital Ratio.

12. The following balances were extracted from the books of Power Ltd on 31 May 1999. The Authorised Share Capital is 250,000 €1 Ordinary Shares.

(A) You are required to prepare the company's Profit and Loss and Appropriation Account for the year ended 31 May 1999 and Balance Sheet as at that date.

	€
Gross Profit	94,000
Rent Receivable	15,600
Bank Overdraft	9,300
Long Term Bank Loan	40,000
Insurance	7,600
Wages	16,000
Carriage Outwards	2,300
Advertising	2,200
Loan Interest	2,000
Cash	2,000
Reserves (Profit and Loss Balance)	2,500
Issued Share Capital	170,000
Machinery	94,000
Buildings	150,000
Furniture and Fittings	44,000
Debtors	16,400
Creditors	17,100

You are given the following information as at 31 May 1999:
  (i) Closing Stock €14,000
  (ii) Rent Receivable Prepaid €3,200
  (iii) Insurance Due €1,400
  (iii) Dividend Declared 3%
  (iv) Depreciation: Furniture and Fittings 10%, Machinery 15%

(B) The Gross Profit of €94,000 in 1999 was down 20% on that of 1998. Calculate the Gross Profit figure for 1998.

13. The following Trial Balance was extracted from the books of Penney Ltd on 31 May 2000. The Authorised Share Capital is 450,000 €1 Ordinary Shares.

TRIAL BALANCE

	DR €	CR €
Purchases and Sales	48,000	199,000
Sales Returns	4,000	
Carriage Inwards	4,600	
Commission Received		4,000
Debtors and Creditors	22,000	13,000
Dividends Paid	11,200	
Buildings	280,000	
Machinery	95,000	
Motor Vehicles	60,000	
Bank Overdraft		2,400
Cash	1,200	
Insurance	8,400	
Wages	27,000	
Issued Share Capital 280,000 €1 Ordinary Shares		280,000
Reserves (Profit and Loss Balance)		71,000
Opening Stock 01 June 1999	8,000	
	569,400	569,400

(A) Prepare the company's Trading, Profit and Loss and Appropriation Account for the year ended 31 May 2000 and a Balance Sheet as at that date.

You are given the following information as on 31 May 2000:
  (i) Closing Stock €11,000
  (ii) Carriage Inwards Due €800
  (iii) Wages Due €7,000
  (iv) Insurance Prepaid €1,400
  (v) Depreciation Machinery 8%, Motor Vehicles 12.5%

(B) Calculate the rate of dividend paid to the shareholders of Penney Ltd. Show your workings.

14. The following Trial Balance was extracted from the books of O'Connor Ltd on 31 May 2000. The Authorised Share Capital is 350,000 €1 Ordinary Shares.

TRIAL BALANCE

	DR €	CR €
Purchases and Sales	52,000	184,000
Returns	1,000	2,000
Carriage Inwards	2,500	
Interest Received		4,000
Dividends Paid	3,600	
Issued Share Capital 120,000 €1 Ordinary Shares		120,000
Insurance	5,600	
Office Expenses	6,200	
Wages and Salaries	29,000	
Opening Stock	11,000	
Reserves (Profit and Loss Balance)		32,700
Debtors and Creditors	6,000	8,000
Machinery	180,000	
Motor Vans	40,000	
Rent	16,000	
Bank Overdraft		2,400
Cash	200	
	353,100	353,100

(A) You are required to prepare the company's Trading, Profit and Loss and Appropriation Account for the year ended 31 May 2000 and a Balance Sheet as at that date.

You are given the following information as on 31 May 2000:
  (i) Closing Stock €13,000
  (ii) Carriage Inwards Due €500
  (iii) Insurance Prepaid €400
  (iv) Rent Due €2,000
  (v) Depreciation: Machinery 8%, Motor Vans 15%

(B) Calculate the Rate of Stock Turnover.

Chapter 3
Club Accounts

The Final Accounts of a club are:

1. **Bar Trading Account.**
2. **Income and Expenditure Account.**
3. **Balance Sheet.**

3.1 Receipts and Payment Account

FIGURE 2 – LAYOUT OF RECEIPTS AND PAYMENT ACCOUNT

RECEIPTS AND PAYMENTS ACCOUNT

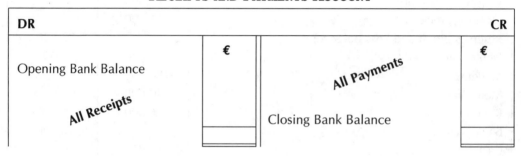

The Receipts and Payments Account for a club is like a Bank Account in a Business.

The **Opening Balance** is the amount of money in the Club at the start of the year.

Notes

1. Many entries in the Receipts and Payments Account will also appear in the Club's

   Bar Trading Account

   Or

   Income and Expenditure Account

2. Adjustments e.g.

   Insurance Prepaid

   Wages Due

   Subscriptions Prepaid

   are not entered in Receipts and Payments Account.

3. Depreciation of Assets are not entered in the Receipts and Payments Account.

4. The main purpose of the Receipts and Payments Account is to show all Receipts and Payments and to calculate the amount of money in the club at the end of the year.

Worked Example

(A) Prepare a Receipts and Payments Account from the following information for the Sky Golf Club:

	€
Bank Balance 01 Jan. 1997	4,300
Subscriptions	60,000
Purchase of Equipment	15,000
Sale of Equipment	4,000
Bar Sales	40,000
Bar Purchases	22,000
Bar Expenses	8,000
Wages of Groundsman	30,000
Insurance	4,000
Office Expenses	4,300

Table 18 — Receipts and Payments Account of Sky Golf Club year ended 31 December 1997

RECEIPTS AND PAYMENTS ACCOUNT

DR					CR
		€			€
01 Jan. 1997	Balance	4,300		Purchase of Equipment	15,000
	Subscriptions	60,000		Bar Purchases	22,000
	Sale of Equipment	4,000		Bar Expenses	8,000
	Bar Sales	40,000		Wages of Groundsman	30,000
				Insurance	4,000
				Office Expenses	4,300
			31 Dec. 1997	Balance c/d	25,000
		108,300			108,300
01 Jan. 1998	Balance b/d	25,000			

(B) Show the above Receipts and Payments Account in an analysed form under the followings headings:

Debit (Receipts) Side: Bank, Subscriptions, Bar, Other Receipts
Credit (Payments) Side: Bank, Bar, General Expenses, Purchase of Assets

Table 19 – Analysed Receipts and Payments Account of Sky Golf Club year ended 31 December 1997

ANALYSED RECEIPTS AND PAYMENTS ACCOUNT

CR		Bank	Sub-scriptions	Bar	Other Receipts			Bank	Bar	General Expenses	Purchase of Assets DR
01 Jan. 1997	Balance	4,300					Purchase of Equipment	15,000			15,000
	Subscription	60,000	60,000				Bar Purchases	22,000	22,000		
	Sale of Equipment	4,000			4,000		Bar Expenses	8,000	8,000		
	Bar Sales	40,000		40,000			Wages of Groundsman	30,000		30,000	
							Insurance	4,000		4,000	
							Office Expenses	4,300		4,300	
						31 Dec. 1998	Balance c/d	25,000			
		108,300	60,000	40,000	4,000			108,300	30,000	38,300	15,000
01 Jan. 1998	Balance b/d	25,000									

3.2 Income and Expenditure Account

The Income and Expenditure Account is like a Profit and Loss Account in a business.

Notes

1. It includes adjustments e.g.
    Subscriptions Due
    Insurance Paid in Advance
    and includes Depreciation.

2. It does not include the purchase or sale of an asset.
3. Sometimes a Bar Trading Account can be prepared before the Income and Expenditure Account. This is usually done when there is an Opening Bar Stock and Closing Bar Stock in the question. In this case Bar Gross Profit is included under Income. Bar Gross Loss is included under Expenditure.
4. The Net Profit in a Club is called the Excess of Income over Expenditure.
5. Accumulated Fund is the Capital of a Club for the Balance Sheet.

Worked Example

(A) Prepare an Income and Expenditure Account for the year ended 31 December 1997.
(B) Show separate Bar Trading Account.
(C) Prepare a Balance Sheet as at 31 December 1997.
(D) Prepare a Treasurer's Report for the A.G.M.

Table 19 – Trial Balance of Sky Golf Club, year ended 31 December 1997

TRIAL BALANCE

	DR €	CR €
Clubhouse	80,000	
Bar Sales		64,000
Bar Purchases	35,000	
Furniture and Fittings	18,000	
Machinery	12,000	
Subscriptions		19,220
Profit on Raffle		3,000
Insurance	2,200	
Wages	12,000	
Light and Heat	2,400	
Accumulated Fund		80,000
Stock for Bar 01 Jan. 1997	3,600	
Repairs to Machinery	600	
Telephone	420	
	166,220	166,220

The following must also be taken into consideration:
  (i) Subscriptions in Advance 31 December 1997 €600
 (ii) Subscriptions Due 31 December 1997 €50
(iii) Bar Stock 31 December 1997 €4,800
 (iv) Insurance Prepaid €400
  (v) Telephone Due €80
 (vi) Depreciation: Machinery 10%

Table 20 – Bar Trading Account of Sky Golf Club, year ended 31 December 1997

BAR TRADING ACCOUNT FOR THE YEAR ENDED 31 DECEMBER 1997

	DR €	CR €
Sales		64,000
Less cost of sales		
Opening Stock	3,600	
Purchases	35,000	
Goods available for sale	38,600	
Less Closing Stock	4,800	
Cost of Sales		33,800
Gross Profit		30,200

Table 21 — Income and Expenditure Account for Sky Golf Club, year ended 31 December 1997

INCOME AND EXPENDITURE ACCOUNT FOR THE YEAR ENDED 31 DECEMBER 1997

	€	€	€
Income			
Bar Gross Profit			30,200
Subscriptions		19,220	
Less Subscriptions in Advance		600	
		18,620	
Add Subscriptions Due		50	18,670
Profit on Raffle			3,000
Total Income			51,870
Less Expenditure			
Insurance	2,200		
Less Insurance Prepaid	400	1,800	
Wages		12,000	
Light and Heat		2,400	
Repairs to Machinery		600	
Telephone	420		
Telephone Due	80	500	
Depreciation: Machinery 10%		1,200	
Total Expenditure			18,500
Excess of Income over Expenditure			33,370

Table 22 – Balance Sheet for Sky Golf Club, year ending 31 December 1997

BALANCE SHEET AS AT 31 DECEMBER 1997

Fixed Assets	Cost	Depreciation to Date	Net Book Value
Clubhouse	80,000		80,000
Furniture and Fittings	18,000		18,000
Machinery	12,000	1,200	10,800
	110,000	1,200	108,800
Current Assets			
Bar Closing Stock		4,800	
Subscriptions Due		50	
Insurance Prepaid		400	
		5,250	
Current Liabilities			
Subscriptions in Advance	600		
Telephone Due	80	680	
			4,570
			113,370
Financed By:			
Accumulated Fund		80,000	
Excess of Income over Expenditure		33,370	
			113,370

Notes

1. *Subscriptions Due*

   This money is owed to the Club and is therefore a Current Asset.

2. *Subscriptions in Advance*

   This is money that has been paid too soon to the club and is therefore a Current Liability.

3. *Telephone Due*

   This is a bill yet to be paid by the club and is therefore a Current Liability

Practice Questions

For questions 1-6 prepare:
  (i) A Receipts and Payments Account
  (ii) An Income and Expenditure Account
  (iii) A Treasurer's report

1. Grange Golf Club for year ended 31 December 1989.

	€
Cash at Bank 01 Jan. 1989	3,400
Subscriptions	40,000
Income from Sponsorship	980
Sale of Lawnmower	400
Sale of Refreshments	2,300
Insurance	6,200
Wages of Green Keepers	16,900
Purchase of Lawnmower	4,800
Purchase of Fertilizers	1,720
Affiliation Fees Paid	2,480
Repainting of Outhouse	6,900
Purchase of Refreshments	1,800
Accountant's Fees	380

2. Wilton Table Tennis Club for the year ended 31 December 1989.

	€
Cash at Bank 01 Jan. 1989	220
Membership Fees (subscriptions)	400
Income from Christmas Draw	3,600
Purchase of Tables	1,150
Cost of Travel to Competitions	400
Affiliation Fees	60
Loss of Entry for Regional Competition	30
Rent of Hall	200
Insurance	344
Cost of Annual Social	460
Income from Annual Social	380
Advertising	290
Cost of Christmas Draw	1,300
Accountant's Fees	90

3. The Abbey Chess Club for the year ended 31 December 1989.

	€
Cash at Bank 01 Jan. 1989	60
Purchase of Chess Boards and Pieces	220
Subscriptions	200
Rent of Room	500
Insurance	60
Entry Fees to Club for Competition Held	390
Costs of Competition	90
Post and Stationery	34
Secretary's Expenses	25
Income from Sponsored Cycle	900
Refreshments for Insured Sponsored Cycle	81
Depreciation on Chess Boards and Pieces	22
Subscriptions Due	10
Donations Received	30

4. The Tallaght Athletic Club year ended 31 January 1989.

	€
01 Feb. 1989 Balance at Bank	420
Purchase of Land	49,000
Bank Loan Received	30,000
Income from Development Draw	6,300
Cost of Development Draw	47,200
Interest on Bank Loan	4,720
House to House Collection	9,208
Advertising	1,145
Insurance	240
Members Subscriptions	842
Income from Flag Day	1,784
Bank Charges	34
Postage and Stationery	83
Purchase of Equipment	1,150
Depreciation on Equipment	4%
Gate Receipts at Sports Days	24
Cost of Sports Day	174
Cost of Entry to Competitions	147
Transport Costs	535

5. Bluerock Card Playing Club for the year ended 31 December 1988.

	€
Cash at Bank 01 Jan. 1988	44
Members Subscriptions	120
Charge on Members for Weekly Card Game	153
Purchase of Tables and Playing Cards	124
Advertising	40
Insurance	74
Postage and Stationery	16
Heat and Light	34
Depreciation on Equipment	12
Postage Stamps on Hand	2
Subscriptions Due	4
Donation to Charity	40
Income from Draw	516
Prize Money Paid	250

6. Donnybrook Billiards Club for year ended 30 June 1989

	€
Bank Balance 01 July 1988	2,900
Rent of Buildings	1,150
Heating	218
Light	93
Insurance	324
Purchase of Billiard Tables	4,300
Depreciation of Billiard Tables	1,200
Subscriptions	3,940
Subscriptions in Advance	40
Subscriptions Due	480
Postage and Stationery	56
Stock of Postage Stamps on Hand	4
Printing of Membership Cards	60

7. The following are the Assets and Liabilities of The Lough Hockey Club on 01 January 1989.

	€
Land and Clubhouse	60,000
Equipment	8,000
Bank	690
Bank Loan	25,000
Accumulated Fund	43,690

Cash and Cheque Transactions for 1989

Balance 01 Jan. Bank	690
Purchase of Jerseys	140
Cost of Cutting Playing Fields	540
Cost of Transport	440
Membership Fees	180
Income from Concert	1,800
Advertising	80
Secretary's Expenses	40
Treasurer's Expenses	30
Painting of Clubhouse	40

Additional information on 31 December:
 (i) Depreciate Equipment 10%
 (ii) Secretary's Expenses Due €25

(A) Prepare:
   (i) A Receipts and Payment Account
   (ii) An Income and Expenditure Account for the year ended 31 December 1989
   (iii) A Balance Sheet as at 31 Dec. 1989
   (iv) A Treasurer's Report

NB Closing Receipts and Payments Account Balance will be a current asset.

8. The following are the Assets and Liabilities of Jersey Football Club on 01 January 1988.

	€
Land and Premises	80,000
Tractor and Lawnmower	6,000
Equipment	3,000
Bank Loan	15,000
Bank	430
Accumulated Fund	74,430

Cash and Cheque Transactions for the year.

Bank Balance 01 Jan. 1988	430
Cleaning of Jerseys	150
Purchase of Jerseys	200
Repairs to Lawnmower	430
Wages of Groundsman	4,640
Team Travelling Expenses	1,280
Insurance	440
Interest on Bank Loan	1,500
Annual House to House Collection	900
Income from Christmas Draw	1,860
Advertising	220
Membership Fees	500
Gate Receipts of Matches	1,980
Income from Cake Sale	620
Income from Sponsored Cycle	2,016
Profit from Sale of Snacks	5,700

Additional Information 31 December 1988:
  (i) Advertising Due €30
 (ii) Insurance Prepaid on 31 Dec. €55
(iii) Depreciation: Tractor and Lawnmower 15%, Equipment 20%

(A) Prepare:
     (i) A Receipts and Payments Account
     (ii) An Income and Expenditure Account for the year ended 31 December 1988
     (iii) A Balance Sheet as at 31 December 1988
     (iv) A Treasurer's Report

9. The following are the Assets and Liabilities on 01 January 1987 of the Wilton Rugby Club.

	€
Playing Fields and Dressing Rooms	120,000
Clubhouse	180,000
Tractor and Lawnmower	4,800
Bank Loan	10,000
Bank	2,641
Accumulated Fund	297,441

Cash and Cheque Transactions for the year.

Bank Balance 01 Jan. 1987	2,641
Repairs on Tractor	130
Wages of Groundsman	6,900
Insurance	3,620
Secretary's Expenses	130
Treasurer's Expenses	15
Audit Fees	290
Telephone	290
Net income from Club Bar	11,040
Membership Fees	1,200
Income from Fund Raising Draw	34,000
Costs of Draw	16,220
Interest on Bank Loan	1,200

Additional Information on 31 December 1987:
  (i) Telephone Due €48
 (ii) Insurance Prepaid €400
(iii) Subscriptions Due €160
 (iv) Subscriptions Paid in Advance €40
  (v) Depreciate Tractor and Lawnmower 20%

(A) Prepare:
    (i) A Receipts and Payments Account
   (ii) An Income and Expenditure Account for the year ended 31 Jan. 1988
  (iii) A Balance Sheet as at 31 Dec. 1988
   (iv) A Treasurer's Report for the A.G.M.

10. Below are the Assets and Liabilities of the Salt Lake Squash Club as at 01 January 1997.

	€
Premises	120,000
Bank	2,640
Equipment	800
Accumulated Fund	123,440

Cash and Bank Transactions for the year.

Bank Balance 01 Jan. 1987	2,640
Heating and Light	4,700
Income from Lighting Meters	10,260
Membership Fees	1,200
Cost of Competition	240
Income from Competition	80
Advertising	60
Income from Sponsorship	414
Insurance	2,600
Bank Interest Received	130
Secretary's Expenses	30
Audit Fees	160

Additional Information on 31 December.
  (i) Stock of Heating Oil on Hand €120
 (ii) Subscriptions Due €80
(iii) Subscriptions Paid in Advance €120
 (iv) Insurance Prepaid €220
  (v) Secretary's Expenses Due €15
 (vi) Depreciation: Equipment 5%

(A) Prepare:
     (i) A Receipts and Payments Account
     (ii) An Income and Expenditure Account for the year ended 31 December 1987
     (iii) A Balance Sheet as at 31 December 1987
     (iv) A Treasurer's Report

11. Below are the Assets and Liabilities of the Midleton Golf Club as at 01 January 1989.

	€
Clubhouse	90,000
Land	200,000
Equipment	50,000
Bank Loan	40,000
Bar Stock	11,460
Accumulated Fund	311,460

Cash and Bank Transactions for year.

Members Subscriptions	119,000
Wages of Groundsman	11,400
Insurance	13,510
Bar Purchases	48,230
Bar Sales	83,000
Heating and Lighting	5,420
Green Fees Received	12,460
Purchase of Lawn Fertilizer	6,300
Water Rates	7,500
Maintenance of Watering System	2,400
Repainting of Clubhouse	22,000
Purchase of Lockers	18,000
Secretary's Expenses	1,800
Postage and Telephone	1,250
Accountant's Fees	1,300
Interest on Bank Loan	6,000
Net Expenditure on Competitions	7,400
Advertising	600
Donation to Charity	250

Additional Information on 31 December 1989:
  (i) Closing Bar Stock €6,400
 (ii) Depreciation: Equipment 20%, Clubhouse 2%
(iii) Insurance Prepaid €1,100
 (iv) Water Rates Due €2,500

(A) Prepare:
       (i) A Receipts and Payments Account
      (ii) A Bar Trading Account
     (iii) An Income and Expenditure Account for the year ended 31 December 1987
      (iv) A Balance Sheet as at 31 December 1987
       (v) A Treasurer's Report

Exam-Type Questions

1. The Treasurer of the Clonmel GAA Club has prepared the following Receipts and Payments for the year ended 31 December 1996.

RECEIPTS AND PAYMENTS ACCOUNT FOR THE YEAR ENDING 31 DECEMBER 1996

DR		€			CR €
01 Jan. 1995	Balance b/f	12,100		Travel Expenses	4,600
	Bar Sales	44,600		Insurance	2,100
	Subscriptions	4,800		Bar Purchases	22,300
	Gate Receipts	2,100		Secretary's Expenses	400
	Income from Raffle	3,200		Purchase of Equipment	9,300
				Expenses of Raffle	600
				Donation to Charity	300
				Balance c/d	27,200
		66,800			66,800
	Balance b/d	27,200			

The following information should also be taken into consideration:
   (i) Subscriptions Prepaid €50
  (ii) Insurance Prepaid €200
 (iii) Depreciate Equipment 10% per annum
 (iv) Bar Stock 01 Jan. 1993 €4,000
   (v) Bar Stock 31 Dec. 1993 €5,000

(A) Prepare:
      (i) A Bar Trading Account
     (ii) An Income and Expenditure Account

(B) From all the information available in the accounts, list three main points that you think should be included in the Treasurer's Report for the A.G.M.
(C) If the Accumulated Fund is €16,100 prepare a Balance Sheet as at 31 December 1996.

2.

TRIAL BALANCE

	DR €	CR €
Clubhouse	30,000	
Equipment	4,000	
Members' Subscriptions		8,300
Insurance	2,400	
Light and Heat	1,800	
Telephone	400	
General Expenses	500	
Profit on Raffle		700
Petty Cash	30	
Bank	2,870	
Accumulated Fund		33,000
	42,000	42,000

Adjustments:
  (i) Depreciation: Equipment 10%
 (ii) Insurance Prepaid €200
(iii) Light and Heat Due €50

(A) Prepare:
      (i) An Income and Expenditure Account for the year ended 31 December 1996
      (ii) A Balance Sheet as at 31 December 1996

(B) From all the information in the accounts list three main points which should be included in the Treasurer's Report.

3. The Treasurer of the Capagh Golf Club has prepared the following Receipts and Payments Account for the year ended 31 December 1995.

RECEIPTS AND PAYMENTS ACCOUNT

DR		€			CR €
01 Jan. 1995	Balance b/d	16,800		Wages of Greenkeepers	32,000
	Subscriptions	64,000		Bar Purchases	49,320
	Bar Sales	72,600		Purchase of Equipment	14,600
	Green Fees Received	12,260		Secretary's Expenses	1,500
	Competition Receipts	4,000		Advertising	200
				Competition Prizes	2,800
				Insurance	5,700
				Light and Heat of Clubhouse	2,600
			13 Dec. 1995	Balance c/d	60,940
		169,660			169,660

You are given the following additional information on 31 December 1995:
- (i) Bar Stock 01 Jan. 1995 €4,600, Bar Stock 31 Dec. 1995 €5,400
- (ii) Insurance Prepaid €1,200
- (iii) Advertising Due €50
- (iv) Subscriptions Due €1,600
- (v) Depreciate Equipment 15% per annum

(A) Prepare:
- (i) A Bar Trading Account for the year ended 31 December 1995
- (ii) An Income and Expenditure Account for the year ended 31 December 1995

(B) The club is planning to start to build a €200,000 extension in two years time. What courses of action should it undertake to raise the necessary money?

4. You have been asked to prepare the accounts for the local Handball Club.

(A) Prepare:
    (i) An Income and Expenditure Account for the year ended 31 December 1995
    (ii) A separate Bar Trading Account for the year ended 31 December 1995
    (iii) A Balance Sheet as at 31 December 1995

TRIAL BALANCE AS AT 31 DECEMBER 1995

	DR €	CR €
Accumulated Fund (01 Jan.1995)		29,500
Clubhouse	30,000	
Equipment	3,800	
Members' Subscriptions		9,600
Bar Purchases	5,680	
Furniture	2,500	
Bar Sales		8,200
Painting of Clubhouse	840	
Light and Heat	240	
Insurance	480	
Bar Stock (1 Jan. 1995)	720	
Postage and Stationery	140	
Wages	4,000	
Profit on Draw		1,100
	48,400	48,400

Additional information on 31 December 1995:
  (i) Bar Stock 31 December 1995 €630
  (ii) Insurance Due €120
  (ii) Subscriptions Due €300
 (iv) Depreciation: Equipment 10%, Furniture 4%

(B) From the information available in the accounts list three main points which you think should be included in the Treasurer's Report for the A.G.M.

5. The Green Glen Golf Club makes cash payments for small amounts that are recorded in a Petty Cash Book.

The following transactions took place during the month of March:

		€
01 Mar.	Received imprest for the month by cheque	150
03 Mar.	Bought postage stamps (voucher no 14)	4
05 Mar.	Donation to charity (voucher no. 15)	10
06 Mar.	Posted parcel (voucher no. 16)	4
07 Mar.	Bought refreshments for office (voucher no. 17)	5
08 Mar.	Bought stationery (voucher no. 18)	8
14 Mar.	Bought cleaning materials (voucher no. 19)	6
16 Mar.	Posted parcel (voucher no. 20)	2
18 Mar.	Paid cleaner's wages (voucher no. 21)	19
20 Mar.	Repairs to computer (voucher no. 22)	12

(A) Complete and balance the Petty Cash Book for the month of March using the following analysis columns. Postage, Stationery, Cleaning, Other Expenses.

(B) Show the posting of the totals of the analysis columns to their accounts in the ledger. Use the accounts provided at the end of this question.

(C) Where would the petty cash balance be shown in the final accounts?

POSTAGE ACCOUNT 8

Date	Details	€	Date	Detail	€

STATIONERY ACCOUNT 9

Date	Details	€	Date	Details	€

CLEANING ACCOUNT 10

Date	Details	€	Date	Details	€

OTHER EXPENSES ACCOUNT 11

Date	Details	€	Date	Details	€

6.

TRIAL BALANCE

	DR €	CR €
Bar Sales		44,000
Bar Purchases	28,000	
Buildings	140,000	
Furniture and Fittings	16,000	
Profit on Raffle		2,500
Machinery	8,000	
Repairs to Machinery	400	
Subscriptions		9,400
Stock for Bar 01 Jan. 1990	4,200	
Postage	160	
Insurance	1040	
Wages	60,00	
Light and Heat	900	
Accumulated Fund		148,800
	204,700	204,700

The following must also be taken into consideration:
  (i) Subscriptions in advance €600
 (ii) Bar Stock 31 Dec. 1990 €6,400
(iii) Insurance Prepaid €200
(iv) Depreciate Buildings 2%, Machinery 15%, Furniture and Fittings 5%

(A) Prepare:
        (i) A Bar Trading Account for year ended 31 December 1990
       (ii) An Income and Expenditure for Buildings same period
      (iii) A Balance Sheet as at 31 Dec. 1990

7.

TRIAL BALANCE

	DR €	CR €
Club Shop Sales		63,000
Club Shop Purchases	31,400	
Club Shop Wages	11,000	
Stock for Shop 01 Jan. 1991	8,100	
Buildings	90,000	
Playing fields	140,000	
Bank Loan		60,000
Members' Subscriptions		900
Transport Costs	7,000	
Insurance	2,500	
Machinery	6,000	
House to House Collection		2,400
General Expenses	3,500	
Accumulated Fund		173,200
	299,500	299,500

The following must also be taken into consideration:
- (i) Club Shop Stock 31 Dec. 1991, €7,400
- (ii) Provide for Interest on Bank Loan 12%
- (iii) Subscriptions Due €50
- (iv) Insurance Prepaid €400
- (v) Depreciation: Machinery 10%

(A) Prepare:
-    (i) A Shop Trading and Profit and Loss Account for the year ended 31 December 1991
-    (ii) An Income and Expenditure Account for the same period.
-    (iii) A Balance Sheet as at 31 Dec. 1991
-    (iv) A Treasurer's Report for the A.G.M.

8.

TRIAL BALANCE

	DR €	CR €
Buildings	120,000	
Machinery	10,000	
Telephone	1,000	
Insurance	2,500	
Bank Loan		40,000
Interest on Bank Loan	600	
Bar Sales		64,000
Bar Purchases	38,000	
Bar Stock 01 Jan. 1992	7,000	
Subscriptions		40,000
Repairs to Machinery	2,000	
Bar Wages	18,000	
General Expenses	12,000	
Accumulated Fund		67,100
	211,100	211,100

You are given the following information as at 31 December 1992:
  (i) Bar Stock 31 Dec. 1992 €9,500
 (ii) Subscriptions Due €2,000
(iii) General expenses Due €1,000
 (iv) Depreciation: Machinery 15%

(A) Prepare
     (i) A Bar Trading and Profit and Loss Account for the year ended 31 December 1992
    (ii) An Income and Expenditure Account for the year ended 31 December 1992
   (iii) A Balance Sheet as at 31 December 1992
   (iv) A Treasurer's Report for A.G.M.

9.

TRIAL BALANCE

	DR €	CR €
Insurance	2,200	
Bank Loan		80,000
Bar Sales		75,000
Bar Purchases	38,000	
Subscriptions		100,000
Green Fees Received		30,000
Interest on Bank Loan	9,000	
Clubhouse and Land	250,000	
Machinery	8,000	
Bar Wages	22,000	
Telephone	400	
Bar Stock 01 Jan. 1993	4,000	
General Expenses	24,000	
Accumulated Fund		72,600
	357,600	357,600

You are given the following information as at 31 December 1993.
  (i) Bar Stock 31 Dec. 1993 €5,500
 (ii) Subscriptions in Advance €3,000
(iii) Insurance Prepaid €400
 (iv) Telephone Due €140
  (v) Depreciation: Machinery 10%

(A) Prepare:
    (i) A Bar Trading and Profit and Loss Account for the year ended 31 December 1993
   (ii) An Income and Expenditure Account for the year ended 31 Dec. 1993
  (iii) A Balance Sheet as at 31 Dec. 1993
   (iv) A Treasurer's Report for the A.G.M.

10.

TRIAL BALANCE

	DR €	CR €
Clubhouse	50,000	
Insurance	1,000	
Subscriptions		2,400
Cash	100	
Bank	1,600	
Secretary's Expenses	600	
Treasurer's Expenses	150	
Bank Loan		40,000
Bank Interest	5,000	
Profit on Sale of Refreshments		4,500
Repairs	400	
Telephone	460	
Transport Costs	700	
Money from Sponsorship		4,800
Accumulated Fund		8,310
	60,010	60,010

Adjustments 31 December 1994:
  (i) Insurance Prepaid £200
  (ii) Subscriptions Prepaid £100
  (iii) Secretary's Expenses Due £150
  (iv) Telephone Due £160
  (v) Depreciation: Clubhouse 2%

(A) Prepare:
    (i) An Income and Expenditure Account for the year ended 31 December 1994
    (ii) A Balance Sheet as at 31 December 1994
    (iii) A Treasurer's Report for the A.G.M.

11.

TRIAL BALANCE

	DR €	CR €
Clubhouse	80,000	
Land	120,000	
Furniture	15,000	
Machinery	12,000	
Equipment for Office	3,000	
Office Expenses	4,000	
Subscriptions		100,000
Insurance	6,000	
Wages	36,000	
Bank	2,000	
Bank Loan		140,000
Bank Interest	21,000	
Repairs	15,000	
Accumulated Fund		74,000
	314,000	314,000

Adjustments 31 December 1995:
 (i) Wages Due €7,000
 (ii) Subscriptions Due €2,000
 (iii) Depreciation: Furniture 5%, Machinery 15%, Office Equipment 10%

(A) Prepare:
   (i) An Income and Expenditure Account for the year ended 31 December 1995
   (ii) A Balance Sheet as at 31 December 1995
   (iii) A Treasurer's Report for the A.G.M.

12. Illen Rowing Club has prepared the following Receipts and Payments Account for year ended 31 December 1996.

RECEIPTS AND PAYMENTS ACCOUNT

CR		€			DR €
01 Jan. 1996	Balance	14,234		Telephone	795
	Subscriptions	9,800		Light and Heat	1,326
	Raffle Income	4,974		Bar Purchases	5,800
	Sale of Equipment	13,500		Insurance	3,100
	Bar Sales	8,700		Purchase of Premises	35,000
31 Dec.1997	Balance c/d	5,813		Manager's Wages	11,000
		57,021			57,021
			01. Jan. 1998	Balance b/d	5,813

(A) Prepare the Club's Income and Expenditure Account for the year ended 31 December 1997 taking the following into consideration:
  (i) Subscriptions Prepaid on 31 Dec. 1996 were €600
  (ii) Telephone Bill Due on 31 December 1996 €134
  (iii) The Club is owed €300 in respect of Bar Sale
  (iv) Depreciation to be charged on Premises at 2% per annum

(B) The club has a surplus of income for the year yet it had a cash shortage on the 31 December 1996. Give a reason for this.
(C) Name two duties of the chairperson of a club.
(D) Explain the following terms:(i) Agenda (ii) Minutes.
(E) Name the official whose duty it is to look after the financial affairs of a club.
(F) Give two advantages to the club of having a Bank Current Account.

NB Include Bar Sales in Income and Expenditure Account in this question (also Bar Purchases).

13. The Treasurer of the Blackpool Hurling Club has prepared the following Receipts and Payments Account for the year ending 31 December 1998.

RECEIPTS AND PAYMENTS ACCOUNT

CR		€			DR €
	Bar Sales	61,420	01 Jan. 1998	Balance b/f	4,260
	Sale of Tractor	6,970		Purchase of New Tractor	27,200
	Subscriptions	9,400		Travel Expenses	9,120
	Raffle Income	8,960		Insurance	3,640
				Purchases of Bar Stock	33,220
				Raffle Prizes	2,600
				Office Expenses	1,800
				Balance c/d	4,910
		86,750			86,750
31 Dec. 98	Balance b/f	4,910			

The following information should also be taken into consideration:
- (i) Subscriptions Due €150
- (ii) Travel Expenses Due €240
- (iii) Office Expenses Prepaid €200
- (iv) Depreciate New Tractor 12.5%
- (v) Bar Stock 01 Jan. 1998 €3,900, Bar Stock 31 Dec. 1998 €4,600

(A) Prepare:
- (i) A Bar Trading Account
- (ii) An Income and Expenditure Account for the year ended 31 December 1998

(B) How much Cash did the Club have on 31 Dec. 1998?

(C) Name two duties of the Club Treasurer.

(D) Name a suitable system of record keeping/bookkeeping that the Treasurer should use for recording the club's daily payments and daily receipts.

(E) When do the club members get an opportunity to question the financial affairs/final accounts of the club?

14. The following information was prepared by the Treasurer of the Clonmel Hurling Club for the year ended 31 December 1999.

	€
Cash in Hand	560

PAYMENTS

Light and Heat	530
Purchase of Lawnmower	5,500
Raffle Prizes	780
Insurance	840
Travel Expenses	6,800

RECEIPTS

Gate Receipts	7,250
Membership Fees	1,800
Raffle Income	8,400

Additional Information
  (i) Membership Fees Due 31 Dec. 1999 €20
 (ii) Insurance Prepaid on 31 Dec. 1999 €120
(iii) Lawnmower to be depreciated 10% per annum

(A) Prepare:
    (i) A Receipts and Payments Account
    (ii) An Income and Expenditure Account for the year ended 31 Dec. 1999 from the information above
    iii) A Balance Sheet as at 31 December 1999. Accumulated Fund is €560

(B) How much cash did the club have on 31 Dec. 1999?
(C) Explain depreciation. State one cause of depreciation.

Chapter 4
Ratios

Useful Terms and Definitions

1. Working Capital $\quad = \quad \dfrac{\text{Current Assets}}{\text{Current Liabilities}}$

2. Acid Test or Liquid Asset $\quad = \quad \dfrac{\text{Current Assets - Closing Stock}}{\text{Current Liabilities}}$

3. Average Stock $\quad = \quad \dfrac{\text{Opening Stock + Closing Stock}}{2}$

4. Stock Turnover $\quad = \quad \dfrac{\text{Cost of Sales}}{\text{Average Stock}}$

5. Return on Capital Employed $\quad = \quad \dfrac{\text{Net Profit}}{\text{Capital Employed}} \times 100$

6. Gross Profit %
    or Gross Profit Margin $\quad = \quad \dfrac{\text{Gross Profit}}{\text{Sales}} \times 100$

7. Net Profit % or Net Profit Margin $\quad = \quad \dfrac{\text{Net Profit}}{\text{Sales}} \times 100$

8. Rate of Dividends = Dividend Rate as % of Issued Share Capital

9. Retained Earnings = Net Profit - Dividends

10. Solvent: Total Assets > External Liabilities
    (External Liabilities = Current Liabilities + Long Term Liabilities)

11. Overtrading: Current Liabilities > Current Assets

12. Period of Credit given to Debtors: $\dfrac{\text{Debtors}}{\text{Credit Sales}} \quad \begin{array}{l} \times \ 12 \ \text{(months per year)} \\ 365 \ \text{(days per year)} \end{array}$

13. Period of Credit
    Received from Creditors $\quad = \quad \dfrac{\text{Creditors}}{\text{Credit Purchases}} \quad \begin{array}{l} \times \ 12 \ \text{(months per year)} \\ 365 \ \text{(days per year)} \end{array}$

14. Shareholders Funds = Issued Share Capital + Reserves

Sample Exam Questions

1.

(A) Explain two limitations of Final Accounts and Balance Sheets in assessing a business.

(B) Examine the Final Accounts and Balance Sheets of Del Ltd for the years 1995 and 1996 set out below. Compare and comment on the performance of the company for the two years using the following ratios:

   (i) Gross Profit Margin
   (ii) Return on Capital Employed
   (iii) Acid Test (quick) Ratio
   (iv) Rate of Dividend Paid

1995

Trading, Profit and Loss and Appropriation Account for the year ended 30 April 1995	€
Sales	180,000
Gross Profit	85,000
Net Profit	54,000
Dividends Paid	17,600
Reserves	36,400

Balance Sheet as at 31 April 1995	€	€
Fixed Assets		180,000
Current Assets (Including Closing Stock €5,200)	28,400	
Less Current Liabilities	22,000	6,400
		186,400
Financed By: 100,000 €1 Ordinary Shares		100,000
Reserves		36,400
Long Term Liabilities		50,000
		18,6400

1996

Trading, Profit and Loss and Appropriation Account for the year ended 30 April 1996	€
Sales	240,000
Gross Profit	98,000
Net Profit	57,000
Dividends Paid	17,400
Reserves	39,600

Balance Sheet as at 31 April 1996	€	€
Fixed Assets		200,000
Current Assets (Including Closing Stock €8,300)	35,900	
Less Current Liabilities	19,900	16,000
		216,000
Financed By: 100,000 €1 Ordinary Shares		100,000
Reserves		76,000
Long Term Liabilities		40,000
		216,000

2. Assume you are Sean Walsh Financial Consultant of 20 Youghal Road, Cork. Study the Financial Accounts and Balance Sheets of Brown Ltd Cork set out below for the years 1996 and 1997. Prepare a Report using today's date for the shareholders of Brown Ltd comparing the performance of the company in the two years under the following three headings:

(i) Profitability   (ii) Liquidity   (iii) Dividend Policy

1993

Trading, Profit and Loss and Appropriation Accounts for the year ended 30 Apr. 1985	
	€
Sales	160,000
Less Cost of Sales	96,000
Gross Profit	64,000
Less Expenses	33,400
Net Profit	30,600
Less Dividends	3,260
Reserves	27,340

1994

Trading Profit and Loss and Appropriation Accounts for the year ended 30 Apr. 1985	
	€
Sales	340,000
Less Cost of Sales	150,000
Gross Profit	190,000
Less Expenses	67,300
Net Profit	122,700
Less Dividends	40,000
Reserves	82,700

Balance Sheet as at 30 April 1985		
	€	€
Fixed Assets		260,000
Current Assets	35,000	
Less Current Liabilities	45,660	-10,660
		249,340
Financed by:		
Ordinary Share Capital		200,000
Reserves		27,340
Long Term Loan		22,000
		249,340

	€	€
Fixed Assets		274,000
Current Assets	96,080	
Less Current Liabilities	48,040	48,040
		322,040
Ordinary Share Capital		200,000
Reserves		110,040
Long Term Loan		12,000
		322,040

3. Light Ltd has an Authorised Share Capital of 250,000 £1 Ordinary Shares. The following information is available for the year ended 31 December 1995.

Sales	250,000	Expenses	70,000
Cost of Sales	110,000	Issued Share Capital	200,000
Capital Employed	340,000	Closing Stock	15,000
Current Liabilities	15,000	Dividends Declared	4%
Debtors	12,000	Opening Stock	7,000

(A) Assume you are Garreth Fitzgerald, Financial Consultant, 4 The Square Thurles Co Tipperary. Prepare a report for the shareholders of Light Ltd on today's date showing the following:
  (i) Gross Profit Margin
  (ii) Amount of Extra Capital Light Ltd can raise from issuing shares
  (iii) Return on Capital Employed
  (iv) The amount Light Ltd had in the bank if the Working Capital Ratio was 3:1
  (v) Profit retained by Light Ltd on 31 Dec. 1995
  (vi) Stock Turnover

4.

(A) State two reasons why a business would prepare a Cash Flow Forecast.

(B) Below is a partially completed Cash Flow Forecast of Hickey Ltd. You are required to complete this form for the months of September, October, November and December, as well as the total columns.
  The following information should be taken into account:
  (i) Wages and Advertising are expected to remain the same every month.
  (ii) Monthly sales are expected to increase by 20% beginning in September.
  (iii) Monthly purchases are expected to increase by 25% beginning in November.
  (iv) The loan repayments will cease after October.
  (v) The shareholders are to invest an additional €60,000 in the business in November.
  (vi) Land is expected to be sold in October for €80,000.
  (vii) New machinery costing €90,000 will be purchased in November.
  (viii) A European Union (EU) grant of €40,000 for equipment is expected in December.

(C) Hickey Ltd forgot to allow for repairs to machinery of €6,000 during this period. State how this omission will affect the net cash position at the end of December.

CASH FLOW FORECAST FOR HICKEY LTD FOR PERIOD JULY - DECEMBER 1998.

	July €	Aug. €	Sep. €	Oct. €	Nov. €	Dec. €	Total for July-Dec. €
Payments							
Sales	60,000	60,000					
Share Capital	—	—					
Land	—	—					
EU Grant	—	—					
A – Total Receipts	60,000	60,000					
Payments							
Wages	5,000	5,000					
Purchases	27,000	27,000					
Advertising	1,400	1,400					
Insurance	—	1,250					
Loan Repayments	3,600	3,600					
Motor Vehicles	—	30,000					
New Machinery							
B – Total Payments	37,000	68,250					
C – Net Cash							
(A - B)	23,000	-8,250					
D – Opening Cash	-8,000	15,000	6,750				
Closing Cash C - D	15,000	6,750					

5. Below is a partially completed Cash Flow Statement of Tobin Ltd. You are required to complete this form for the months of March, April, May and June as well as all the Total columns.

The following information should be taken into account:
   (i) Monthly sales are expected to rise by 25% beginning in April.
   (ii) A European Union (EU) grant of €25,000 for equipment is expected in June.
   (iii) The shareholders are to invest an additional €60,000 in the business in April.
   (iv) Light and Heat is expected to decrease by 75% in May.
   (v) Rent and Wages are expected to remain the same every month.
   (vi) A new advertising campaign during April will cost €15,000.
   (vii) Another motor vehicle will be purchased in April at a cost of €25,000.
   (viii) New equipment costing €80,000 will be purchased in May.
   (ix) Purchases will increase by 20% beginning in May.

(B) State two important pieces of information which Tobin Ltd can obtain from this Cash Flow Statement.

(C) Tobin Ltd forgot to allow for overtime payments of €4,000 for the period. State how this omission will affect the Net Cash position at the end of June.

CASH FLOW STATEMENT OF TOBIN LTD FOR THE PERIOD JANUARY - JUNE 1996

Jan. – June	Jan. €	Feb. €	Mar. €	Apr. €	May €	June €	Total for €
Receipts							
Sales	48,000	48,000					
EU Grant							
Share Capital							
A — Total Receipts	48,000	48,000					
Payments							
Light and Heat	2,000	—					
Rent	600	600					
Wages	3,000	3,000					
Advertising							
Motor Vehicles	30,000	—					
New Equipment							
Purchases	25,000	25,000					
B – Total Payments	60,600	28,600					
C – Net Cash							
A - B	-12,600	+19,400					
D Opening Cash	4,000	-8,600	10,800				
Closing Cash C + D	-8,600	10,800					

6.

	€		Calculate:
Sales	90,000	(i)	% Mark-Up on Cost
Purchases	48,000	(ii)	Gross Profit Margin
Opening Stock	11,000	(iii)	Average Stock
Closing Stock	7,000	(iv)	Rate of Stock Turnover
Expenses	30,000	(vi)	Cost of Sales
Issued Share Capital	100,000	(vii)	Gross Profit
Proposed Dividends	5%	(viii)	Net Profit
		(ix)	Retained Earnings

For questions 6-11 it may be necessary to do a Trading Profit and Loss and Appropriation Account – in some cases working backwards from NET Profit & Expenses = Gross Profit & Cost of Sales = Sales and filling in other missing entries accordingly.

7.

	€		Calculate:
Fixed Assets	100,000		
Current Assets	60,000	(i)	Dividends
Current Liabilities	40,000	(ii)	Working Capital Ratio
Opening Stock	6,000	(iii)	Acid Test Ratio
Closing Stock	8,000	(iv)	Net Profit
Issued Share Capital	100,000	(v)	Gross Profit
Bank Loan	10,000	(vi)	Sales
Retained Earnings	10,000	(vii)	Goods available for sale
Dividend	5%	(viii)	Purchases
Expenses	45,000	(ix)	Stock Turnover
Cost of Sales	40,000	(x)	Return on Capital Employed
		(xi)	Shareholder's Funds

Hint: Start at end of Profit & Loss Appropriation Account with Retained Earnings & Dividends = Net Profit & Expenses = Gross Profit.

8.

	€		Calculate:
Sales	84,000		
Purchases	52,000	(i)	Dividends
Opening Stock	7,000	(ii)	Working Capital Ratio
Closing Stock	8,000	(iii)	Acid Test Ratio
Expenses	17,000	(iv)	Net Profit
Issued Capital	80,000	(v)	Gross Profit
Proposed Dividends	6%	(vi)	Retained Earnings
Current Assets	40,000	(vii)	Average Stock
Current Liabilities	20,000	(viii)	Rate of Stock Turnover
		(ix)	Shareholder's Funds

9.

	€		Calculate:
Current Assets	36,000		
Current Liabilities	12,000	(i)	Rate of Stock Turnover
Opening Stock	8,000	(ii)	Purchases (Hint: Prepare Trading Account and find missing entry).
Closing Stock	6,000		
Cost of Sales	60,000		
Sales	90,000	(iii)	Working Capital Ratio
Issued Share Capital	120,000	(iv)	Acid Text Ratio
Rate of Dividends	3%	(v)	Amount of Dividend
Expenses	15,000	(vi)	Net Profit

10.

	€		Calculate:
Fixed Assets	140,000	(i)	Net Assets
Current Assets	80,000	(ii)	Working Capital
Current Liabilities	40,000	(iii)	Working Capital Ratio
Closing Stock	20,000	(iv)	Liquid Asset Ratio
(Credit) Sales	150,000	(v)	Stock Turnover
Debtors	30,000	(vi)	Gross Profit
(Credit) Purchases	100,000	(vii)	Net Profit
Creditors	25,000	(viii)	Return on Capital
Opening Stock	10,000		Employed
Cost of Sales	90,000	(ix)	Period of Credit given to
Expenses	20,000		Debtors
Capital Employed	180,000	(x)	Period of Credit Received
			from Creditors

(B) If a 5% depreciation of Fixed Assets was omitted from the Accounts what is the correct Net Profit?

11.

	€		Calculate:
Sales	80,000	(i)	Percentage Mark-Up on
Purchases	35,000		Cost
Opening Stock	10,000	(ii)	Gross Profit Margin
Closing Stock	15,000	(iii)	Average Stock
Expenses	25,000	(iv)	Rate of Stock Turnover
Issued Share Capital	120,000	(v)	Cost of Sales
Proposed Dividends	5%	(vi)	Gross Profit
		(vii)	Net Profit
		(viii)	Retained Earnings

12. Bright Ltd has an Authorised Share Capital of 300,000 £1 Ordinary Shares. The following information is available for the year ended 31 December 1999.

	€
Sales	280,000
Expenses	80,000
Cost of Sales	120,000
Issued Share Capital	250,000
Capital Employed	400,000
Closing Stock	15,000
Current Liabilities	30,000
Dividends Declared	5%
Debtors	20,000

(A) Assume you are Ann Hayes, Financial Consultant, 6 The Square, Thurles. Prepare a report for the shareholders of Bright Ltd on today's date showing the following:

  (i) Gross Profit Margin
  (ii) Return on Capital Employed
  (iii) Amount of extra capital Bright Ltd can raise from issuing shares
  (iv) Profit retained by Bright Ltd at 31 Dec. 1999
  (v) Amount Bright Ltd had in the bank if the Current Ratio is 2.5:1

(B) R. Brown has 8,000 shares in Bright Ltd.
  (i) How much will he receive in the form of dividends?
  (ii) Do you think he would be satisfied? Give one reason for your answer.

13. Clear Ltd has an Authorised Share Capital of 280,000 £1 Ordinary Shares. The following information is available for the year ended 31 December 2000

		€
(i)	Sales	340,000
(ii)	Opening Stock	15,000
(iii)	Cost of Sales	150,000
(iv)	Issued Share Capital	240,000
(v)	Expenses	100,000
(vi)	Capital Employed	420,000
(vii)	Current Liabilities	40,000
(viii)	Dividends Declared	4%
(ix)	Closing Stock	25,000
(x)	Debtors	40,000

Calculate:
  (i) Gross Profit Margin
  (ii) Return on Capital Employed
  (iii) Amount Clear Ltd can raise in extra capital from issuing shares
  (iv) Profit retained by Clear Ltd at 31 Dec. 2000
  (v) Rate of Stock Turnover
  (vi) Amount Clear Ltd has in Bank if Current Ratio is 2:1

Chapter 5
Bank Reconciliation Statements

The **Bank Account** (or **Cash Book**) is the account holder's own record of money received and spent.

The **Bank Statement** is the Bank's Record of money received an spent by the account holder.

The Bank Statement will include entries such as:

Bank Charges

There is a small fee charged by the Bank for each transaction from a Current Account for writing cheques, ATM transactions etc.

Bank Interest Charged

This is interest charged by the Bank on Bank Overdrafts. The customer of the Bank will not know the exact amount of interest, until such time as the customer receives the Bank statement from the Bank.

Standing Order (S/O)

A Standing Order is where an account holder gives permission to his/her Bank to make regular fixed payment from his/her account.

Direct Debit (D/D)

A Direct Debit is where you give written permission to a business to request your Bank to make fixed or variable payments to them from time to time.

Credit Transfer

Credit Transfer, also known as Bank Giro, is a means by which money can be paid directly into your Bank Account by another person.

Dishonoured Cheque

This is a cheque that you the customer has received and lodged to your account, but the Bank of the person who wrote the cheque will not honour the cheque (has refused to honour) due to insufficient funds in the account of the drawer (the person who wrote the cheque). Such cheques are sometimes marked R/D meaning refer to drawer i.e. go back to the person who paid you by this cheque.

The account holder should have these documented in his/her Bank Account (Cash Book) until the Bank Statement is received from the Bank. The account holder uses the Bank Statement to balance his/her own account and prepare a revised cash book. The revised cash book is the most up-to-date, true record of the account but it may still differ from the Bank Statement due to:

(a) *Cheques Drawn not Presented for Payment*
Cheques issued by the account holder are recorded in his/her personal records but will not appear on the account holder's bank account until it is presented for payment. In this case the Bank's record is better than the account holder's record.

(b) *Lodgements not Credited by the Bank*
If the account holder lodges money to his/her account late on the last day of the month the lodgement may not appear on his/her next Bank Statement if the Bank has already prepared this earlier in the day.

A **Bank Reconciliation Statement** is then prepared to reconcile the two records and to check for errors.

Worked Example

T. Osborne had a balance of €240 in his Business Bank Account on 01 December 1996. His transactions for the month of December were as follows:

03 Dec.	Paid Motor Van Insurance	(cheque no. 684)	€590
04 Dec.	Cash Sales Lodged		€800
05 Dec.	Withdrew by ATM		€60
29 Dec.	Paid Telecom	(cheque no. 685)	€90
31 Dec.	Cash Sales lodged		€200

At the end of December T. Osborne received the following Bank Statement from the Bank.

BANK STATEMENT

Date	Details	DR	CR	Balance
		€	€	€
01 Dec	Balance			240
04 Dec	Lodgement		800	1,040
05 Dec	ATM	60		980
08 Dec	Direct Debit E.S.B.	94		886
10 Dec	Credit Transfer by Debtors		320	1,206
11 Dec	Cheque no.684	590		616
31 Dec	Bank Charges	6		610

CASH BOOK (BANK ACCOUNT)

DR		€			CR €
01 Dec.	Balance	240	03 Dec.	Motor Van Insurance	
				Cheque no. 684	✓590
04 Dec.	Sales	✓800	05 Dec.	ATM	✓60
31 Dec.	Sales	x 200	29 Dec.	Telecom Cheque no. 685	x 90
			Dec. 31	Balance c/d	500
		1,240			1,240
01 Jan.	Balance b/d	500			

Revised Cash Book		Revised Bank Account	
Balance	500	Direct Debit E.S.B.	94
Credit Transfer	320	Bank Charges	6
		Balance c/d	720
	820		820
Balance b/d	720		

Bank Reconciliation Statement		
Balance as per Revised Cash Book		720 DR
Add Cheque drawn not presented for payment		90
		810
Less lodgement not credited		200
Balance as per Bank Statement		610 CR

Summary

1 Prepare Cash Book Bank Account

2 Compare Cash Book with the Bank Statement by putting a ✓ on entries that appear in both the Cash Book and Bank Statement, and an **X** on entries that appear only in one or the other.

3 Prepare a Revised Bank Account bringing existing Bank Account up to date with the entries marked with an **X** in Bank Statement.

4 Prepare a Bank Reconciliation Statement.

1.

Q1 (A) Explain three types of security that a bank would accept when giving a businessman a loan for his Private Limited Company.

(B) (i) Explain what is meant by a Dishonoured Cheque.

(ii) Give two reasons why a Bank will dishonour a cheque.

(C) Fenton Ltd opened a current account in the Trustees Savings Bank on 01 June 1995 and lodged €800 to the account. The following transactions took place in the month of June.

	€
03 June Purchased Stock (cheque no. 1)	480
04 June Paid Advertising (cheque no. 2)	110
05 June Paid Rates (cheque no. 3)	300
06 June Paid Rent (cheque no. 4)	150
12 June Lodged to account	800
04 June Cash Sales Lodged	2,400
26 June Paid Creditor (cheque no. 5)	1,600
30 June Paid E.S.B. (cheque no. 6)	120
30 June Cash Sales lodged	300

Fenton Ltd received the following Bank Statement on 30 June 1995.

BANK STATEMENT

Date	Details	DR	CR	Balance
		€	€	€
01 June 1996	Lodgement		800	800
05 June 1996	Cheque no. 1	480		320
08 June 1996	Cheque no. 2	110		210
09 June 1996	Cheque no. 3	300		90 OD
12 June 1996	Lodgement		800	710
14 June 1996	Lodgement		2,400	3,110
14 June 1996	Cheque no. 4	150		2,960
20 June 1996	Bank Giro		620	3,580
22 June 1996	Standing Order Insurance	400		3,180
30 June 1996	Bank Charges	30		3,150

(i) Prepare Fenton's Bank Account for the month of June

(ii) Compare the balance in Fenton Ltd's bank account with that in the Bank Statement and make whatever adjustments that are necessary to Fenton Ltd's bank account i.e. A Revised Bank Account.

(iii) Prepare a Bank Reconciliation Statement.

2. Margaret Buckley opened a current account in the Bank of Ireland on 01 July 1994. On 01 July 1994 she lodged €600 to the account. The following are the transactions for the month of July:

	€
03 July 1994 Paid E.S.B. (cheque no. 1)	48
07 July 1994 Lodged to her account	150
08 July 1994 Purchased clothes (cheque no. 2)	120
09 July 1994 Withdrew by ATM card	40
10 July 1994 Purchased groceries (cheque no. 3)	60
18 July 1994 Withdrew by ATM card	50
26 July 1994 Purchased groceries (cheque no. 4)	80
31 July 1994 Lodged to her account	150

(A) Write up Margaret's own record of her bank transactions for July showing the closing balance

(B) Compare Margaret's own records with the Bank Statement she received (below). Make whatever adjustments necessary to Patricia's own records i.e. A Revised Bank Account, and then prepare a Bank Reconciliation Statement.

BANK STATEMENT No. 1 31 JULY 1994

Date	Details	DR	CR	Balance
1994		€	€	€
01 July	Lodgement		600	600
06 July	Cheque no. 1	48		552
07 July	Lodgement		150	702
09 July	ATM	40		662
11 July	Cheque no. 2	120		542
18 July	ATM	50		492
20 July	Standing Order	200		292
22 July	Credit Transfer		100	392
30 July	Bank Charges	5		387

(C) State three items that could be included under Bank Charges.

(D) What considerations will a Bank manager take into account before deciding to give a person a loan?

3. Thomas Wright has a current account with Bank of Ireland. He received the Bank Statement below on 30 April 1996.

BANK OF IRELAND CURRENT ACCOUNT				

Thomas Wright,
116 O'Connell Street,
Dungarvan,
Co Waterford

BRANCH CODE

STATEMENT NUMBER

DATE

ACCOUNT NUMBER

Date	Details	DR	CR	Balance
1996		€	€	€
01 Apr.	Balance			1,160
07 Apr.	Cheque no. 208	140		1,020
10 Apr.	Cheque no. 207	130		890
11 Apr.	Cheque no. 210	200		690
13 Apr.	Credit Transfer		150	840
16 Apr.	Standing Order	260		580
18 Apr.	Direct Debit	92		488
20 Apr.	ATM	140		348
28 Apr.	Current Account Fees	8		340

(A) Why are the cheque numbers not in sequence? Explain your answer.
(B) Explain the main difference between a direct debit (DD) and a standing order (S/O) as a means of making payments.
(C) List three items which could appear under Current Account Fees.
(D) Compare Thomas Wright's own records below with the Bank Statement he received from the Bank. Make whatever adjustments necessary to Thomas's own records and then prepare a Bank Reconciliation Statement.

BANK ACCOUNT T. WRIGHT'S OWN RECORDS

DR						CR
		€				€
01 Apr.	Balance	1,160	02 Apr. 2	Telecom (cheque no. 207)		130
30 Apr.	Lodgement	300	03 Apr.	County Council (cheque no. 208)		140
			06 Apr.	Burke Ltd (cheque no. 209)		160
			10 Apr.	E.S.B. (cheque no. 210)		200
			20 Apr.	ATM		140
			30 Apr.	Balance c/d		690
		1,460				1,460
01 May	Balance b/d	690				

4. Mary Fitzgerald opened a current account in the Midlands Bank when she lodged €600 to the account on 01 July 1993. The following are her transactions for the month of July.

	€
01 July Lodgement	600
01 July Paid Rent (cheque no. 1)	160
03 July Withdrew by ATM	60
06 July Lodgement	600
08 July Paid Insurance (cheque no. 2)	140
10 July Withdrew by ATM	50
14 July Purchased Furniture (cheque no. 3)	500
16 July Purchased Computer (cheque no. 4)	1,200
20 July Lodgement	1,200
31 July Lodgement	600

BANK STATEMENT NO. 1 DATE: 31 JULY 1995

Date	Details	DR	CR	Balance
1995		**€**	**€**	**€**
01 July	Lodgement		600	600
02 July	Cheque no. 1	160		440
03 July	ATM	60		380
06 July	Lodgement		600	980
10 July	ATM	50		930
18 July	Cheque no. 4	1,200		270 OD
20 July	Lodgement		1,200	930 CR
21 July	Bank Giro		300	1,230
22 July	Cheque no. 3	500		730
24 July	Standing Order	400		330
26 July	Bank Interest	3		327
28 July	Bank Charges	7		320

(A) Write up Mary Fitzgerald's Cash Book (Bank Account) for the month of July showing the closing cash balance.

(B) Compare Mary Fitzgerald's own Cash Book records with the Bank Statement of 31 July 1995 and prepare a Revised Cash Book.

(C) Prepare a Bank Reconciliation Statement.

5. Seamus Kierney opened an account in the South East Bank PLC on 1 September 1996 when he lodged €800 to a current account. The following are his transactions for the month of September.

	€
01 Sept. Purchased Office Equipment (cheque no. 1)	900
02 Sept. Paid Insurance (cheque no. 2)	460
04 Sept. Withdrew by ATM	100
07 Sept. Lodgement	800
22 Sept. Paid Travel Company (cheque no. 3)	700
23 Sept. Lodgement	800
24 Sept. Withdrew by ATM	100
25 Sept. Purchased Computer (cheque no. 4)	900
26 Sept. ATM Withdrawal	200
30 Sept. Lodgement	800

SOUTH EAST BANK DUNGARVAN

BANK STATEMENT No. 1 30 SEPTEMBER 1996

Date	Details	DR	CR	Balance
1996		€	€	€
01 Sept.	Lodgement		800	800
04 Sept.	ATM	100		700
06 Sept.	Cheque no. 1	900		200 DR
07 Sept.	Lodgement		800	600
13 Sept.	Cheque no. 2	460		140
23 Sept.	Lodgement		800	940
24 Sept.	ATM	100		840
24 Sept.	S/O	600		240
26 Sept.	Cheque no. 4	900		660 DR
26 Sept.	ATM	200		860 DR
28 Sept.	Bank Interest	4		864 DR
29 Sept.	Current Account Fees	20		884 DR

(A) Prepare Seamus Kierney's own records of his Bank Account for the month of September.

(B) Compare Seamus Kierney's own records of his Bank Account with the Bank Statement and prepare a Revised Bank Account.

(C) Prepare a Bank Reconciliation Statement.

6. R. Halpin had a balance in his current account of €240 on 01 October 1996. The following were his transactions for the month of October.

		€
02 Oct.	Withdrew by ATM	40
04 Oct.	Purchased Petrol (cheque no. 1)	16
05 Oct.	Purchased Clothes (cheque no. 2)	80
07 Oct.	Lodgement	200
09 Oct.	Withdrew by ATM	60
14 Oct.	Lodgement	200
17 Oct.	Paid Car Insurance (cheque no. 3)	260
21 Oct.	Lodgement	200
24 Oct.	Paid Telecom (cheque no. 4)	160
31 Oct.	Lodgement	200

BANK STATEMENT 31 OCTOBER 1996

Date	Details	DR	CR	Balance
1996		€	€	€
01 Oct.	Balance			240
02 Oct.	ATM	40		200
03 Oct.	Bank Interest	15		185
04 Oct.	Bank Giro		260	445
07 Oct.	Lodgement		200	645
09 Oct.	ATM	60		585
14 Oct.	Lodgement		200	785
15 Oct.	Cheque no. 2	80		705
16 Oct.	D/D	200		505
17 Oct.	Cheque no. 1	16		489
20 Oct.	Bank Charges	21		468
21 Oct.	Lodgement		200	668

(A) Prepare R. Halpin's own records of his Cash Book for the month of October.

(B) Compare R. Halpin's own records with the Bank's records in the Bank Statement and then prepare a Revised Cash Book.

(C) Prepare a Bank Reconciliation Statement.

7. D. McGrath had a balance of €200 in his Bank Account in the Tipperary Bank Ltd on 01 September 1995. The following were his transactions for the month of September.

	€
01 Sept. Withdrew by ATM	60
03 Sept. Purchased groceries (cheque no. 87)	44
04 Sept. Purchased heating oil (cheque no. 88)	220
09 Sept. Withdrew by ATM	70
11 Sept. Purchased petrol (cheque no. 89)	25
14 Sept. Lodged wages to account	760
17 Sept. Withdrew by ATM	90
25 Sept. Purchased groceries (cheque no. 90)	70
28 Sept. Purchased furniture (cheque no. 91)	820
30 Sept. Lodged wages to account	760

BANK STATEMENT 30 SEPTEMBER 1995

Date	Details	DR	CR	Balance
1995		€	€	€
01 Sept.	Balance			200
01 Sept.	ATM	60		140
06 Sept.	Cheque no. 88	220		80DR
07 Sept.	Cheque no. 87	44		124 DR
09 Sept.	ATM	70		194 DR
14 Sept.	Lodgement		760	566
15 Sept.	Cheque no. 89	25		541
17 Sept.	ATM	90		451
18 Sept.	Bank Giro		150	601
22 Sept.	Bank Charges	6		595
23 Sept.	Bank Interest	10		585

(A) Write up D. McGrath's Cash Book (Bank Account) for the month of September, showing the closing balance.

(B) Compare D. McGrath's own records in the Cash Book with the Bank Statement received from the Bank and prepare a Revised Cash Book (Revised Bank Account).

(C) Prepare a Bank Reconciliation Statement.

8. B. Flynn Ltd had a balance of €220 in his Business Bank Account on 01 November 1995. His transactions for the month of November were as follows:

		€
02 Nov.	Paid for repairs to machinery (cheque no. 563)	1,450
03 Nov.	Cash Sales lodged	640
04 Nov.	Purchased heating oil (cheque no. 564)	450
05 Nov.	Received from debtor, lodged to Account	200
06 Nov.	Paid insurance (cheque no. 565)	940
10 Nov.	Purchased new computer (cheque no. 566)	3,700
26 Nov.	Paid creditor S. Dempsey (cheque no. 567)	800
27 Nov.	Cash Sales lodged	1,100
30 Nov.	Cash Sales lodged	1,600

BANK STATEMENT 30 NOVEMBER 1995

Date	Details	Dr	Cr	Balance
1995		€	€	€
01 Nov.	Balance			220
03 Nov.	Lodgement		640	860
04 Nov.	Cheque no. 564	450		410
05 Nov.	Lodgement		200	610
06 Nov.	Cheque no. 563	1,450		840 DR
08 Nov.	Cheque no. 565	940		1,780 DR
11 Nov.	Cheque no. 566	3,700		5,480 DR
20 Nov.	Bank Interest	40		5,520 DR
21 Nov.	Credit Transfer Bank Giro		2,000	3,520 DR
27 Nov.	Lodgement		1,100	2,420 DR
28 Nov.	Standing Order	440		2,860 DR
30 Nov.	Bank Charges	10		2,870 DR

(A) Prepare Cash Book (Bank Account) for Brian Flynn Ltd for the month of November.

(B) Compare the Cash Book with the Bank Statement sent by the Bank on 30 November and then prepare a Revised Cash Book.

(C) Prepare a Bank Reconciliation Statement.

9. B. Meehan Ltd had an overdraft in his Business Bank Current Account of €700 at 01 January 1996. The following were his Bank Current Account transactions for the month of January 1996.

	€
04 Jan. Paid Telecom (cheque no. 1,641)	194
05 Jan. Lodgement of amount received from Debtors	2,700
07 Jan. Paid wages (cheque no. 1,642)	700
09 Jan. Purchased motor car (cheque no. 1,643)	11,000
10 Jan. Cash Sales lodged	7,000
11 Jan. Paid Car insurance (cheque no. 1,644)	560
20 Jan. Cash Sales lodged	4,000
22 Jan. Paid repairs to office equipment (cheque no. 1,645)	90
26 Jan. Paid Creditor (cheque no. 1,646)	4,800
31 Jan. Lodgement Cash Sales	1,500

BANK STATEMENT 31 JANUARY 1996

Date	Details	DR	CR	Balance
1996		€	€	€
01 Jan.	Balance			700 DR
07 Jan.	Cheque no. 1,641	194		894 DR
05 Jan.	Lodgement		2,700	1,806
07 Jan.	Cheque no. 1642	700		1,106
09 Jan.	Cheque no. 1,643	11,000		9,894 DR
10 Jan.	Lodgement		7,000	2,894 DR
14 Jan.	Cheque no. 1,644	560		3,454 DR
15 Jan.	S/O	200		3,654 DR
20 Jan.	Bank Interest	900		4,554 DR
20 Jan.	Lodgement		4,000	554 DR
21 Jan.	Bank Charges	45		599 DR
24 Jan.	Credit Transfer		5,000	4,401 CR
27 Jan.	Cheque no. 1,646	4,800		399 DR

(A) Prepare a Cash Book for Brendan Meehan Ltd for the month of January.
(B) Compare the Cash Book with the Bank Statement of 31 January and prepare a Revised Bank Account.
(C) Prepare a Bank Reconciliation Statement.

10. Brid Fenton had a current account with the Midland Bank. She received the following statement on 30 November 1997.

Statement of Account with

<table>
<tr><td colspan="5" align="center">**MIDLAND BANK LTD.**
Portlaw Branch Co Waterford.</td></tr>
<tr><td colspan="2">**ACCOUNT HOLDER**
Brid Fenton
Parklane, Portlaw.</td><td colspan="3">**BRANCH CODE** 92-64-31

ACCOUNT NO. 3896

TYPE OF ACCOUNT Current

Statement No. 26</td></tr>
<tr><td></td><td></td><td>**DR**</td><td>**CR**</td><td>**Balance**</td></tr>
<tr><td></td><td></td><td>€</td><td>€</td><td>€</td></tr>
<tr><td>01 Nov.</td><td>Balance</td><td></td><td></td><td>228 DR</td></tr>
<tr><td>04 Nov.</td><td>Cheque no. 431</td><td>60</td><td></td><td>288 DR</td></tr>
<tr><td>10 Nov.</td><td>Lodgement</td><td></td><td>1,300</td><td>1,012</td></tr>
<tr><td>12 Nov.</td><td>ATM</td><td>90</td><td></td><td>922</td></tr>
<tr><td>14 Nov.</td><td>Cheque no. 432</td><td>60</td><td></td><td>862</td></tr>
<tr><td>15 Nov.</td><td>S.O. TSB</td><td>480</td><td></td><td>382</td></tr>
<tr><td>17 Nov.</td><td>Credit Transfer</td><td></td><td>590</td><td>972</td></tr>
<tr><td>19 Nov.</td><td>Cheque 433</td><td>70</td><td></td><td>902</td></tr>
<tr><td>21 Nov.</td><td>D/D E.S.B.</td><td>74</td><td></td><td>828</td></tr>
<tr><td>30 Nov.</td><td>Current Account Fees</td><td>6</td><td></td><td>822</td></tr>
<tr><td>30 Nov.</td><td>Interest</td><td>5</td><td></td><td>817</td></tr>
</table>

(A) Explain what is meant by DR on 01 November.
(B) Explain the appearance of interest on the Bank Statement on 30 November.
(C) Explain the difference between S/O and DD.
(D) Name one use for each of the following:
  (i) ATM Card
  (ii) Cheque Card
(E) The following is Brid's own account of her bank transactions. Compare this Cash Book/Bank Account with the Bank Statement she received from the Bank and then answer (i) and (ii) below.
  (i) Prepare a Revised Cash Book
  (ii) Prepare a Bank Reconciliation Statement

CASH BOOK/BANK ACCOUNT

DR			€		CR		€
10 Nov.	Salary		1,300	01 Nov.	Balance		228
30 Nov.	Children's Allowance		60	01 Nov.	Heating Oil (cheque 432)		60
				02 Nov.	Insurance cheque 431		60
				08 Nov.	ATM		90
				15 Nov.	S/O TSB		480
				17 Nov.	Car Repairs (cheque 433)		70
				24 Nov.	Furniture		
					Store (cheque 434)		200
				Nov 30	Balance c/d		172
			1,360				1,360
01 Dec.	Balance b/d		172				

(F) Make whatever adjustments that are necessary to Brid's own records in your answer book to update her Cash Book/Bank Account.

(G) Prepare a Bank Reconciliation Statement.